THE banh mi HANDBOOK

THE banh mi HANDBOOK

Recipes for Crazy-Delicious Vietnamese Sandwiches

Andrea Quynhgiao Nguyen

PHOTOGRAPHY BY PAIGE GREEN

TEN SPEED PRESS

Berkeley

CONTENTS

seafood

· 71 ·

pork and beef

· 83 ·

vegetarian

· 103 ·

alternative banh mi

· 115 ·

INTRODUCTION

SOME PEOPLE LIKE TO BAKE PIES. I LOVE TO MAKE sandwiches. I've tinkered with them since elementary school. Our family often started the day with Vietnamese sandwiches. My mother would set out baguette or sliced white bread, butter, Vietnamese silky sausage (*gio lua*, page 44), and black pepper. Each person was responsible for toasting his or her bread and assembling a simple banh mi.

Off to school I went, fueled by the combination of protein, fat, and carbohydrates until lunchtime, when I'd tuck into a bologna or liverwurst sandwich that I'd packed for myself. In the mid-afternoon, I'd come home and make a sandwich snack, experimenting with luncheon meats, saltine crackers, and margarine, popular foods of the 1970s. I was a chubby child.

On the weekends, our family often bought banh mi (pronounced "bun mee") in the granddaddy of Vietnamese-American enclaves, Little Saigon located in Southern California's city of Westminster. The two-for-one deals allowed us to score cheap sandwiches for our family of seven. They were a steal (three banh mi for $4!), albeit often made with poor ingredients and little care. We tracked and followed banh mi deals for months, trying different shops that lured us with banners advertising their discount offers. But after hearing my mother say, "*Tien nao cua nay*" ("You get what you pay for") too many times, our family pivoted. We started making our own Saigon-style banh mi loaded with all the bells and whistles.

I practiced preparing mayonnaise while my sisters debated the sweet-tart balance in our daikon and carrot pickle. Mom crafted old-school Vietnamese cold cuts, many of which were wrapped in banana leaf that my brother cut from a tree in our front yard. She updated her pâté via a Julia Child recipe, forgoing pork for chicken livers, which she saved from whole chickens she had prepped for other dishes. We encased our banh mi in excellent baguettes baked by Vietnamese immigrants who'd settled nearby.

This book is my ode to banh mi, my first sandwich love. It's a crazy combination of ingredients—lots of vegetable and some animal, a remarkable display of synergistic textures and flavors. The recipes showcase banh mi's endless possibilities, with nods to the roots of Vietnamese cooking as well as the creativity that propels it forward. Take a look, and cook, and tinker.

what is banh mi?

Whenever you explore the streets of Vietnam or strip malls of a Little Saigon, a thousand snacks beckon. Sticky rice with coconut, tropical fruit smoothies, and deep-fried dumplings vie for your attention, but inevitably, if you're a sandwich lover like me, you succumb to the banh mi vendor. He or she may tantalize you with cold cuts, pickles, and baguettes beautifully displayed on a cart. Or perhaps the line of customers at a bustling banh mi shop piques your interest.

Why not? Everyone enjoys a well-crafted sandwich. And with banh mi, for a modest amount of money, you get to ingest Vietnam's delectable history and culture. The bread, condiments, and some of the meats are the legacy of Chinese and French colonialism. The pickles, cilantro, and chile reflect Viet tastes for bright flavors and fresh vegetables.

The French, who officially ruled Vietnam from 1883 to 1954 but arrived as early as the seventeenth century, introduced baguettes to Vietnam. At first the Viets called the bread *banh Tay* (Western or French bread; *banh* is a generic term for foods made with flours and legumes). It was mainly associated with French foods such as *bo*, *pho-mat,* and *bit-tet*—Vietnamese pidgin terms for French *beurre* (butter), *fromage* (cheese), and *bifteck* (beef steaks). By 1945, the bread had become commonplace enough for its name to switch to *banh mi,* literally meaning bread made from wheat (*mi*). Dropping the *Tay* signaled that the bread had been fully accepted as a Viet food.

People like my parents, born in 1930s northern Vietnam, snacked on freshly baked, fist-shaped rolls simply adorned with salt and pepper. When my father could afford it, he'd spend a few extra cents to add a smearing of liver pâté. My mother was drawn to a vendor who strategically positioned himself outside the school she attended. Most of the sandwiches made in northern Vietnam at that time were simple affairs, just bread, meat and seasonings, without any vegetable additions. That purity contrasted with the action in the south, particularly in Saigon (now Ho Chi Minh City), where cooks were concocting fanciful renditions, reflections of their free-wheeling attitude and living-large lifestyle.

My father's eighty-something-year-old friends recall that around the early 1940s, Saigon vendors started offering *banh mi thit nguoi,* an East-meets-West combination of cold cuts stuffed inside baguette with canned French butter or fresh mayonnaise, pickles, cucumber, cilantro, and chile. Maggi Seasoning sauce, a soy sauce–like condiment likely introduced by the French, was the condiment of choice for adding savory depth. Somewhere along the line, the term *banh mi* came to signal not only bread but the ubiquitous sandwich.

Reunification of North and South Vietnam via the communist takeover in 1975 resulted in a mass exodus of refugees, many of whom settled in North America, France, and Australia; the United States is home to the largest Vietnamese population outside of Vietnam. Those who came from Saigon and the surrounding areas brought fond memories of Saigon-style sandwiches and yearned to savor them once more, and banh mi shops, bakeries, and delis sprung up in response.

Decades after refugees and immigrants brought banh mi to America, the customizable, affordable sandwich is known far beyond the borders of Little Saigon

banh mi or *bánh mì*?

On March 24, 2011, banh mi was added to the *Oxford English Dictionary*. You don't have to italicize it anymore!

neighborhoods. Modern banh mi shops like Baoguette in New York, Baguette Box in Seattle, Bun Mee in San Francisco, and Saigon Sisters in Chicago crank out sandwiches for downtown professionals and hipsters alike. Banh mi food trucks, the modern version of Vietnam's itinerant banh mi street vendors, attract legions of hungry fans. A number of trend-setting chefs have put banh mi on their menus. Meanwhile, outposts of Lee's Sandwiches, a chain of Viet-American delis, as well as mom-and-pop sandwich shops in Little Saigons all over are jumping with business.

Banh mi recipes are showing up in cookbooks, newspapers, magazines, and food television shows. The sandwich made the cover of the July 2012 issue of *Sunset* magazine and *Minnesota Lunch*, a book on the regional food history of the Minneapolis–Saint Paul area. Online chatter about banh mi is plentiful, with countless blog posts, breadless Paleo versions, as well as geeky discussions on how the bread is made.

So while you can enjoy Vietnamese history in a bite of banh mi, you can also interpret its arc as a fine example of global food culture. Banh mi started out as a colonial novelty in Vietnam, became a nationwide favorite, was transported and transplanted via a diaspora, and was enthusiastically adopted by new audiences. Like people in Vietnam, these new fans enjoy banh mi for what it is: a super tasty sandwich.

using this book

My goal here is to inform and inspire your sandwich-making prowess. This book is organized as if you were to open a sandwich shop.

Check out Banh Mi 101 (pages 5 to 11) to understand what goes into the sandwich. The Banh Mi Pantry (pages 7 and 8) lists essential and frequently used ingredients for preparing recipes in this book. The master banh mi recipe gives guidance on timing and advance prep, and the variations will expand your banh mi horizons.

The bread chapter includes a fabulous recipe for homemade banh mi rolls—and tips for finding suitable bread to buy. After these primers are recipe chapters for "keepers"—banh mi components that you can easily make and keep around: mayonnaise, sauces, and pickles.

The accouterments in place, it's time for the main feature: the recipe chapters focus on fillings. Suggestions for using a filling, assembling sandwiches, as well as extra tips and ideas are often in the "Note" section at the end of a recipe. The final recipe chapter is for new-fangled banh mi incarnations.

Before tackling a recipe, review the directions. Each cook's situation varies, so taste, tweak, and take the leap to make a recipe your own. When you make banh mi at home, you can truly call the shots.

banh mi 101

To make a good sandwich, you need to understand how one comes together—the purpose and placement of each ingredient, as well as timing and advance preparation. This chapter dials it in for novices and experienced cooks alike. Along with the master banh mi recipe, here are suggestions for fun, nontraditional banh mi presentations.

banh mi pantry

Do you need exotic ingredients to make excellent banh mi? No. (Surprise!) Most of what's required is practically at your fingertips or readily available at supermarkets, natural foods markets, and specialty grocers—mine the Asian/ethnic food section wherever you shop. However, the best deals on Maggi Seasoning sauce or premium fish sauce are at Chinese and Viet markets. Farm-fresh, local ingredients, if available, give spectacular results.

ESSENTIALS

Bread Be choosy about the bread but don't suffer over it; see page 14 for tips on sourcing bread. Keep it at room temperature for a few days or freeze it for up to a month.

Chiles To lend bright, spicy notes to banh mi, keep 3 or 4 medium-hot chiles (such as jalapeño and Fresno) in the fridge, where they'll stay fresh for a good week. See page 81 for details on chile heat.

Cilantro Fresh herbs contribute zestiness, and cilantro is the default choice. Trim about ½ inch (1.25 cm) from the ends of a bunch, then stand them like a bouquet of flowers in a container of water. Loosely cover with a thin plastic bag and refrigerate. Change the water every 2 or 3 days to keep it perky for a week. To avoid flossing as you eat, coarsely chop the entire sprig. Try herbs like mint and Thai basil (cut up large leaves), or combine with cilantro.

Cucumber Practically any variety will do for refreshing the palate and adding crunch. I prefer English (European) cucumbers because they taste great and don't need peeling. A cucumber keeps well for about 5 days in the fridge. One 8-ounce (225 g) English cucumber is enough for 6 to 8 sandwiches. Remove the seeds before cutting strips or crescents, but leave the seeds when slicing circles or ovals.

Maggi Seasoning Sauce For first-class banh mi, drizzle on Maggi Seasoning sauce; it will boost each bite with an umami hit. At supermarkets, find it near browning sauces and gravy enhancers, or in the Latino food section. Chinese and Viet grocers shelve it with the soy sauces. The standard Chinese version is more robust than the German-made European version. If unavailable, buy Thai-made Golden Mountain soybean sauce at an Asian market, make mock Maggi (page 30), or sub regular soy sauce, tamari, or salt.

Mayonnaise Buy or make mayonnaise (pages 24 to 28). Homemade has a shorter life span, but it tastes infinitely better than store bought. Mayo is most often used to moisten the bread and enrich the filling. If you don't like mayo, keep European-style salted butter on hand (or use avocado in season).

Pickle Stash a jar of pickles (see pages 33 to 37) in the fridge to inject crunch and color. Make a double batch of a favorite one—pickles keep well.

maggi magic

Maggi Seasoning sauce, simply called Maggi by Viet people, is practically synonymous with banh mi. The meaty-tasting, soy sauce–like condiment unifies and adds a distinctive savory note to Vietnamese sandwiches. Maggi was invented in Switzerland in the late 1880s and the French likely brought it to Vietnam, where it became a staple and symbol of European sophistication. Pronounce its name as "MAH-gee" if you want to impress a Viet person.

OFTEN-USED FRESH AROMATICS

Garlic Peel a bunch of garlic cloves and refrigerate in an airtight container for up to 5 days. Prep work goes faster.

Ginger Buy robust, heavy hands of ginger with smooth skin. Refrigerate unpeeled in a plastic bag in the produce bin for weeks.

Lemongrass Look for firm, rigid stalks and check the cut bottoms for freshness. Keep, refrigerated, for up to a week or trim and freeze. See page 37 for prepping tips.

Shallot Because shallots vary in size, use the measurements and weights in the recipes to check quantities. Yellow onion can be substituted in a pinch.

GO-TO SPICES

Chinese Five-Spice Powder This earthy spice blend goes into cold cuts, marinades, and even the Viet sloppy Joes on page 97. Find in supermarkets, spice shops, and Chinese grocers. It should smell savory-sweet, not evocative of apple or pumpkin pie.

Curry Powder Experiment with different blends to find your ideal. If the blend contains salt, hold off on adding salt until the end of cooking.

Pepper Consider keeping a jar of freshly ground black pepper on hand, buying whole peppercorns and using a coffee grinder dedicated to grinding spices (to clean the grinder, grind 2 teaspoons of raw rice).

Salt I mostly use uniodized table salt and fine sea salt, and occasionally kosher salt. If you use kosher, double the quantity in the recipes.

FAVORITE CONDIMENTS AND SEASONINGS

Fish Sauce Use a premium fish sauce for best results. Reliable brands include Red Boat, MegaChef, and Viet Huong. Check ingredient lists if you're gluten sensitive. Look for *nuoc mam nhi* or *nuoc mam cot* on the label to indicate that the first extraction was used—a sign of craftsmanship and good flavor.

Hoisin Sauce Delicate-tasting Lee Kum Kee brand is sold at many supermarkets in the Asian food section; robust Koon Chun brand is mostly available at Chinese and Southeast Asian markets. Both are terrific.

Oyster Sauce Kikkoman's oyster sauce has great briny depth and is stocked at many supermarkets. For Lee Kum Kee brand, use the basic one with the panda label or the more premium one featuring a label of a woman, boy, and oysters in a boat.

Sesame Oil Keep toasted sesame oil in a dark, cool spot; refrigerate if you seldom use it.

Soy Sauce For *regular soy sauce*, use Kikkoman or Pearl River Bridge (light or superior light). *Dark soy sauce* is mostly available at Asian markets. If you don't have it, use the substitute specified in the recipes. Tamari (regular or wheat-free) can stand in for regular soy sauce.

Sriracha Chile Sauce Huy Fong's Rooster brand of Sriracha is a favorite, but there are other contenders. Try Sriracha aïoli (page 26).

Vinegar Invest in a gallon-size bottle of distilled white vinegar and you'll be set for making banh mi pickles. Heinz brand is excellent.

master banh mi

Makes 1 sandwich

This recipe assumes that you've made the main filling already: have everything prepped and your sandwich will come together in a snap. Unless a recipe specifies a particular combination of ingredients, feel free to experiment. As a guideline, a well-balanced banh mi with all the fixings has a visual ratio of 1:1 or 1:2 of main filling to vegetables.

Vegetable Add-Ons (Choose All, Some, or None)

A small handful (¼ cup / 60 ml) of pickled vegetables, drained of brine

3 or 4 thin slices medium-hot chile, such as jalapeño or Fresno (retain the seeds for fire)

4 to 6 cucumber strips, rounds, or ovals, cut ⅛ to ¼ inch (3 to 6 mm) thick

1 to 2 tablespoons coarsely chopped cilantro sprigs, or 1 to 2 tablespoons coarsely chopped fresh herb leaves

Filling (Choose One or More)

About 3 ounces (90 g) total of any filling in this book

Bread (Choose One)

1 homemade banh mi roll (page 17)

Petite baguette

Handspan section of French baguette

Other suitable bread

Fat (Choose One or More)

Mayonnaise (regular or flavored)

Garlic yogurt sauce (page 29)

Salted butter

Avocado slices

Seasoning (Choose One or More)

Maggi Seasoning sauce

Mock Maggi sauce (page 30)

Spicy hoisin sauce (page 31)

Soy sauce or tamari

Salt and pepper

Before assembling the sandwich, prep the vegetable add-ons and set aside. Slice, reheat, sear, or return the filling to room temperature; see individual recipes for guidance.

If needed, recrisp the bread in a toaster oven preheated to 325°F (160°C) for 3 to 6 minutes. Cool for a few minutes or the mayo or butter will melt into a yucky oiliness. (See Notes on page 10 for a nearly miraculous bread revival method.)

Use a serrated bread knife to slit the bread lengthwise, leaving it attached on the back side to hold the sandwich together; it's okay if you accidentally cut all the way through. Use your fingers to remove some of the insides from one or both halves, depending on how much doughiness you want; save the insides to make pâté, page 46. (If you like, cut and hollow out the bread before recrisping.)

Spread your chosen fat on the two cut sides of bread, covering all way to the edge. (If using avocado, lay down thin slices and mash them slightly so they stick to the bread.) Season by drizzling in Maggi or other liquid condiment, or sprinkling on salt and pepper. Working from the bottom up, layer on the filling and the pickle, chile, cucumber, and/or herb. Close the sandwich and use the bread knife to cut in half crosswise. Enjoy.

continued

NOTES

Prep the chile, cucumber, and cilantro up to 2 days in advance and refrigerate in separate airtight containers. Put the cilantro atop a bit of paper towel to absorb moisture.

To revive lifeless or very soft bread, rub the crust with wet hands to lightly moisten, then bake in a toaster oven preheated to 350°F (180 or 175°C) for about 7 minutes, until hot and crisp.

banh mi variations

To vary banh mi for different occasions and needs, just tweak the presentation. For example:

Banh Mi Sliders Use mini hamburger buns or other small rolls. Split and toast the bread, then remove some of the bread from the top half to accommodate the vegetables. Assemble as usual, scaling down to match the size of the buns and rolls. For example, cut the cucumber into thinner rounds, halve or quarter chile slices, and use less pickle and/or cut it up to help the slider hold together. These are ideal for a children's party or light lunch.

Giant Banh Mi Make banh mi using a full-size baguette or ciabatta, then cut it into small sections for a crowd. It's perfect for a Super Bowl–type party.

Open-Face Banh Mi To craft a lower carb banh mi, finish your creation without a top slice of bread but with cucumber slices—these make it easier to hold together. Use a little less vegetable on these or they'll be unwieldy.

Banh Mi Crostini Cut baguette diagonally into thick slices, each about ⅓ inch (8 mm) thick and 4 inches (10 cm) long. If you like, brush on a little olive oil before toasting the bread in a toaster oven until it begins to color, 1 to 2 minutes. Let cool, then smear on mayo or butter, sprinkle a few drops of Maggi, then layer on thin slices of cucumber, filling, pickle, chile, and cilantro—cut the pickle into smaller pieces and halve the chile as necessary. Serve as an appetizer or snack with extra pickle on the side, if you like.

Banh Mi Smorgasbord Terrific for a lazy Sunday brunch or to use leftovers: set out assorted banh mi components and let people compose their own. Toast bread slices, as for crostini, if you wish. Anything goes.

toaster ovens and microwave ovens: banh mi's best friends

These small kitchen appliances are workhorses for making banh mi. A toaster oven heats up quickly for crisping bread and warming a piece of chicken katsu. The microwave oven is terrific for quickly removing the chill from pâté and refreshing fillings. Banh mi shops often have both on hand. Put yours to use.

bread

In Vietnamese, the term *banh mi* means "sandwich," but it also means "bread." They are inextricably linked. After all, you can't have banh mi the sandwich without banh mi the bread.

Finding good bread for banh mi is important, but it doesn't have to be difficult. The bread shouldn't overwhelm or fight with the goodies inside. It complements, receives, and protects. Not all breads should be used for banh mi. However, great banh mi can be made with a variety of breads—if you like, bake it yourself.

bread buying guide

Understanding the rationale behind the bread used for banh mi will get you far in sourcing the best bread. What's typically used is a baguette-style bread, either sections cut from a long one or individual petite-size rolls. It's lightweight and inexpensive, with a delicate crust that practically shatters with each bite. Inside, the airy crumb has a slight sweetness and chewy tenderness. These qualities allow the bread to integrate well with the rich mayo, salty Maggi Seasoning sauce, flavorful fillings, crisp vegetables, sprightly herb, and bright chile.

Brilliant as it is at its job, bread suitable for banh mi is actually humble stuff that's pretty easy to find. Freshly baked bread is best. If you have a Vietnamese enclave nearby, mine it. Banh mi shops will likely sell bread too. Otherwise, use these guidelines.

WHERE TO LOOK

Find banh mi bread at supermarkets, ethnic grocers, bakeries, delis, bodega-style convenience stores, and specialty grocers.

BREAD CHARACTERISTICS

- Feels relatively light when picked up
- Has a delicate (thin) crust
- Possesses a tender, chewy-soft interior (press on it and it should lazily bounce back)
- Tastes faintly sweet
- Is considered everyday, affordable bread

EXAMPLES OF BREADS THAT WORK WELL

- French or Italian rolls or loaves from supermarket bakery departments
- "Baguette" at Chinese or Vietnamese markets, bakeries, and delis
- Mexican bolillo or telera rolls
- Cubano rolls
- Ciabatta rolls or loaves
- Partially baked (parbaked) rolls or loaves of French or Italian (including ciabatta) style bread (follow instructions to finish baking)
- Kaiser rolls
- Hoagie or cheesesteak rolls
- Sandwich bread (white, wheat, multigrain, or gluten-free)
- Mini slider buns

WHAT TO AVOID

Pricey rustic breads with a strong, thick crust and toothsome chew *do not* work well for banh mi. They may scrape the roof of your mouth as you eat and/or overpower the myriad ingredients inside.

CONSIDER HOMEMADE

Instead of buying the bread, you could bake some yourself. The recipe on page 17 produces marvelous rolls for banh mi.

bread recipe backstory

Viet home cooks don't typically bake bread. They can buy it inexpensively and most people lack ovens. But in 2007, after fielding numerous emails about Viet-style baguettes, I published a recipe on my website. It was easy and tasty but frankly, needed improvement. My ultimate aim was reproducing my ideal: a light bread with a crisp crust and cottony crumb. It just took me until now to figure it out.

Why did it take so long? Many Vietnamese professional cooks don't want to discuss their techniques for fear that you'll be their new competition. I tried diplomacy, enlisting my parents to ask around but their queries were ignored. My friend Mike Ly volunteered his family connections with the owners of a Vietnamese bread bakery but their response to my interview request was, "Sorry, no."

I sleuthed and persisted, lurking on TheFreshLoaf.com and watching YouTube videos of Viet cooking demos. To crack the banh mi code, I snapped photos and scrutinized the labels of supermarket baguettes and Mexican bolillos (close kin to Viet banh mi), and perused bread and food science books.

I chatted up professional bakers. One Little Saigon insider divulged that Viet bakeries often employed dough conditioners to obtain a lofty rise. That ingredient is in many commercially produced breads, but it's not readily available to home cooks. I ordered some from King Arthur, and through cookbook author Kate Leahy obtained *mejorante para pan*, a dough improver that her aunt got in Mexico.

Out of the blue, a white middle-age bakery owner from central California attended one of my cooking classes and provided this hint: the key to baking Viet-style bread was *not* using rice flour (it is used to absorb humidity in Vietnam, he said) but rather letting the dough proof to a near full rise before baking.

Then I met chef Bryant Ng and his wife Kim Luu-Ng, owners of The Spice Table in Los Angeles. Like me, the couple had hit walls trying to figure out a bread recipe for their banh mi lunch menu. They luckily found and hired Ngoc Bui, a third-generation banh mi master. Kim arranged for me to spend a morning with him but on the day of our appointment, the bread oven broke down.

Instead, Ngoc recounted his arduous life as a baker. He began learning the trade when he was 14 years old and managed to maintain it over the years, despite the odds. In Vietnam, when an oven wasn't available, he made one by recycling an oil barrel. While detained at a Malaysian refugee camp, he found ingredients and implements to bake banh mi for his Viet compatriots. In Southern California, he opened up his own shop but bad business dealings forced him to walk away. A dapper, proud man in his 50s with graying temples, Ngoc had hands that were stiff from shaping countless baguettes.

We briefly discussed ingredients and he sincerely admitted that there was nothing fancy involved. However, I noticed that his professional-grade flour contained ascorbic acid as a dough conditioner. Ngoc didn't know about dough conditioners. He simply knew his craft. I didn't get a formal banh mi lesson that morning but my determination was renewed. I kept on tinkering until I got satisfaction. For now, that is.

homemade banh mi rolls

Yields 6 rolls · Takes about 2¹/₂ hours, plus 45 minutes for cooling

Years of pondering, and three months of daily baking, led to these exceptional rolls. They have crisp exteriors and fluffy, chewy-tender interiors, the hallmarks of excellent Viet-Franco breads. Plus, they don't need special ingredients or equipment.

To make banh mi rolls, many Viet bakers prepare fast-rising dough with wheat flour that contains a moderate protein level—what you'd use for cookies or Asian dumplings. The loftiness usually comes from dough improvers such as ascorbic acid and enzymes. My substitute for professional-grade dough improver is a combination of vital wheat gluten (VWG) and vitamin C, which I mix with unbleached all-purpose flour and instant (fast acting/rapid rise) yeast. A bit of salt and vegetable shortening further help the bread to be light and airy.

In America, brands that work well include Gold Medal and Whole Foods flour; Crisco, Earth Balance, and Spectrum shortening; SAF/Red Star and Fleischman's yeast; Bob's Red Mill and Giusto's vital wheat gluten; and La Baleine sea salt. Because of its higher protein, King Arthur flour requires only 4 teaspoons (0.4 oz / 12 g) of VWG.

In this recipe, be precise and weigh the ingredients using the metric measurements. For the vitamin C, empty a capsule or crush a tablet into a powder with a knife or mortar and pestle.

500 mg vitamin C from a capsule or crushed tablet

1 teaspoon (0.2 oz / 5 g) fine sea salt

1½ teaspoons (0.2 oz / 6 g) sugar

About 2 teaspoons (0.25 oz / 7 g / 1 envelope) instant dry yeast

2 tablespoons lightly packed (0.6 oz / 18 g) vital wheat gluten, plus more as needed

3 cups plus 3½ tablespoons (16 oz / 454 g) unbleached all-purpose flour, plus more as needed

1½ tablespoons (0.6 oz / 18 g) shortening, in 3 or 4 chunks, at room temperature

1¼ cups (10 oz / 284 g) very warm tap water (about 110°F / 49°C)

MIX AND RISE

Put the vitamin C, salt, sugar, yeast, vital wheat gluten (VWG), and flour in the bowl of a heavy-duty stand mixer (to mix by hand, see Notes, page 21). Put the paddle attachment on the machine. Mix the dry ingredients on the lowest speed for 1 minute, adding the shortening midway. Stop the mixer to add the water. Restart on the lowest speed and continue mixing for about 1 minute to form a shaggy ball around the paddle. Let sit for 5 minutes, uncovered, to hydrate. Lightly oil a bowl for rising the dough. Set aside.

continued

Pull the dough off the paddle, attach the dough hook, and mix on medium-low (speed 2 on a KitchenAid) for 2 minutes, until smooth and medium-firm; with dough improvers in the mix, a long kneading isn't necessary. Under ideal conditions, the dough initially rolls along the walls of the mixer bowl as it is being kneaded by the hook. After about 90 seconds of kneading, the dough gets wrapped around the hook and completely pulls away from the sides of the bowl; a little dough may remain stuck to the bottom of the bowl. If the dough wraps around the hook early on, it's a tad soft, so add 1 to 2 teaspoons of VWG to stiffen and build structure.

Transfer to an *unfloured* work surface and briefly knead into a ball. If the dough feels soft and moist (think perspiration on a humid day), lightly dust the work surface with flour and knead it in. The finished dough should feel barely tacky, like a Post-It note. When pressed, it should immediately bounce back but leave a shallow indentation. Put into the oiled bowl, turn to coat, then tightly cover with plastic wrap. Set in a warm spot, such as an oven with the light on, to rise for 45 minutes, or until doubled.

CUT, ROUND, AND SHAPE

Uncover the bowl and set the plastic wrap aside to reuse later. Invert the bowl onto your work surface to let the dough gracefully fall out. Use a knife to cut it in half, each about 13¾ ounces (390 g). Gently form each half into a brick shape, then cut crosswise into 3 pieces, each about 4½ ounces (128 g). You'll have 6 pieces total.

To round each dough piece, use both hands to cup it, then pull, tuck, and gather the edges toward the center to form a small mound. Aim to create a taut outer surface. Put the mound, seam side down, on your work surface, then loosely cover with the saved plastic. Let rest and rise for 10 minutes. Meanwhile, line a heavy-duty rimmed baking sheet (I use a half sheet pan) with parchment paper. Set aside.

Uncover the mounds and save the plastic (you'll need it one more time). To shape each roll, put the dough smooth side down on your work surface. Press and pat into a big thick disk (like a hamburger patty), about 4¼ inches (10.5 cm) wide and ⅝ inch (1.5 cm) thick. Some gassy bubbles may get popped. Don't worry.

Imagine a scroll that rolls inward from the top and bottom. Roll the top down and over twice, pressing each time with moderately firm pressure along the entire edge to seal the seam well. When done, the top should be rolled to the midline. Now roll the bottom up and over twice, sealing well each time and finishing at the midline. Firmly pinch the top and bottom together to form a seam at the center and create surface tension. Pinch the ends to seal, too.

Gently roll and rock the dough back and forth, stretching it into a torpedo about 6½ inches (16.25 cm) long and 1¾ inches (4.5 cm) wide at the plump center; if the dough feels resistant, let it rest for a few minutes and reroll. Place the roll, seam side down, on the lined baking sheet. Repeat, arranging the rolls in a 3 by 2 formation, roughly 2 inches (5 cm) apart at their middles; the ends will be about 1 inch apart. See the photos opposite for help.

continued

PRESS AND PAT

ROLL DOWN

ROLL UP

PINCH TO SEAL

ROLL AND ROCK

DONE!

PROOF AND BAKE

Smear a little oil or use nonstick spray on 2 pieces of plastic wrap (use the saved one plus a new piece), then loosely cover the rolls with them. Let rise until *more than doubled*, close to a full rise, about 1 hour at moderate room temperature. The rise can happen very quickly in warm weather conditions so if you're concerned, preheat the oven right after shaping the rolls. Regardless, monitor the rolls via these benchmarks:

- At 20 minutes, or when most rolls are 2 inches (5 cm) at the middle, set up the oven for baking. Place a broiler pan or heavy-duty rimmed baking sheet on the oven floor, its rim positioned near the oven edge (this will create steam later; see Notes). Put a rack in one of the lower positions, about 5 inches (12.5 cm) from the water pan, leaving space to later safely pour water into the pan. Place a baking stone (or inverted heavy-duty rimmed baking sheet) on the rack. Preheat to 475°F (245°C / gas mark 9).

- At 45 minutes, or when the rolls have nearly doubled, remove the plastic wrap. Let the rolls dry and finish rising for 10 to 15 minutes. Meanwhile, bring some water (about 1 cup / 240 ml) to a boil, then lower the heat to keep hot. Find a 1-quart (1 l) measuring cup or similar vessel to later pour hot water into the pan in the oven. Partially fill a spray bottle with water. Set aside.

- Around the 1 hour mark, or when the rolls are porpoiselike and 2½ to 2¾ inches (6.25 to 7 cm) at the middle, it's time to bake. Pour a good ½ cup (120 ml) of hot water into the pouring vessel. Set near the stove.

To slash (score) each roll, hold a sharp knife (such as a long boning/fillet knife) nearly horizontal to the roll surface and make one angled cut on the midline; an ideal slash is shallow, ⅛ to ¼ inch (3 to 6 mm) deep. Do it with steady confidence in a smooth, decisive fashion. It's okay to very gently rescore to deepen a slash.

Mist the rolls 5 or 6 times with the spray bottle. Slide the baking sheet onto the stone, carefully pour water into the pan on the oven floor, then close the door. Lower the heat to 425°F (220°C / gas mark 7) and bake for 22 to 24 minutes, or until golden brown and hollow sounding when thumped on the bottom crust. When the rolls are light golden, usually after baking for 15 minutes, rotate the pan and/or shift the rolls to expose them equally to the oven temperature variation. (If the rolls achieve that color after baking for only 10 minutes, lower the temperature to 400°F / 200°C / gas mark 6.)

When done, turn the oven off. Let the rolls further crisp and brown in the oven for 8 to 10 minutes. Cool on a rack for about 45 minutes before eating. The sides will slightly soften. If the rolls are a little flat, don't fret because you'll be filling them to a beautiful plumpness. Use the rolls as is or reheat to a shattering crispness, per the master banh mi recipe on page 9.

NOTES

Guess the protein level of all-purpose (plain) flour by the nutrition information on the label; 3 or 4 grams of protein per 30-gram serving indicates moderate protein; 5 grams of protein per 30-gram serving means a high protein level.

Look for vital wheat gluten (VWG) at natural food stores and well-stocked markets in the baking or bulk section. The light beige powder may be labeled gluten flour, instant gluten flour, or pure gluten flour. VWG is *not* the same as high gluten flour.

Vegetable shortening is a white, vegetable-based fat that is often, but not always, hydrogenated; look for it near the oils or butter. If the shortening is hard at room temperature, melt it, and then cool before using.

Parchment paper (baking or greaseproof paper) is usually sold near aluminum foil.

To mix dough by hand, put all ingredients except the water in a bowl. Stir with a wooden spatula to combine and break up the shortening. Make a well in the center, pour in the water, then stir for about 1 minute to form a ragged ball that wipes the bowl; if extra moisture is needed, dip the spatula in water. Let sit, uncovered, to hydrate for 5 minutes. Transfer to an *unfloured* work surface and knead for 2 to 3 minutes. If necessary, work in extra VWG and/or flour as directed, then continue with the rise.

If the pan for making steam cannot sit on the oven floor, put it on the lowest shelf position. Position another rack on the next rung up for the stone or inverted baking sheet.

When rolls touch and bake as conjoined twins, pry them apart after they've browned a bit. If they don't come apart with minimal jiggling, wait until they are done baking.

When rolls are made in advance, they can be left out for several hours before using. Or cool completely and freeze in a zip-top bag overnight or up to a month; thaw at room temperature and reheat. Stored in plastic at room temperature, the rolls soften like most bread and lose their good looks.

For bigger rolls, decrease the amount of salt. Omit it altogether and the rolls will be extra voluptuous but lack flavor. Or sprinkle extra salt and pepper or Maggi into your banh mi to compensate.

Bake the rolls directly on the stone if you're adventurous. The rise is slightly bigger. Proof the rolls on parchment paper. Keeping the rolls on the paper, use a pizza peel to slide them onto the baking stone.

Make other shapes. Tester Doug Grover baked 2 long baguettes from this dough. I've shaped it into 16 round rolls for banh mi sliders. Adjust the proofing time accordingly. Baking temperature and time are roughly the same.

mayonnaise, sauces, and pickles

This chapter includes recipes for components found in most banh mi: luscious mayonnaise, punchy sauces, and tangy pickles. Store-bought mayonnaise and seasonings make perfectly fine sandwiches, though the pickles need to be home-made (don't worry—they're quick and easy). Add homemade mayonnaise (page 24) and you'll be in banh mi heaven. And if you'd like to venture further, there's plenty more to explore.

homemade mayonnaise

Makes 1 generous cup (250 ml) · **Takes about 5 minutes, plus 30 minutes resting**

Part of the banh mi maker's craft is preparing mayonnaise from scratch. While I do keep a jar of store bought, full-fat mayo in the fridge, when I want the best banh mi possible, I make it. It's easy in a food processor; see Mayo Notes for a blender method. You'll need a measuring cup with a spout to pour the oil.

1 large egg, near or
at room temperature

¼ plus ⅛ teaspoon salt

1 teaspoon Dijon mustard

2 teaspoons water

1 tablespoon fresh
lemon juice

1 cup (240 ml) canola oil

Put the egg, salt, mustard, water, and lemon juice in the food processor's work bowl. Start the processor and after a creamy yellow mixture forms, 5 to 10 seconds, start pouring the oil through the feed tube in a slow, steady stream as thin as angel hair pasta. Midway through, after things thicken, pour a thicker stream, as wide as spaghetti.

After about 2 minutes, all the oil should be incorporated and the mayo should be creamy and spreadable. (If yours is curdled or soupy—broken—see Mayo Notes, opposite.) If needed, adjust with extra salt (savoriness) or lemon juice (tang), pulsing the machine to blend well.

Transfer to an airtight container. Before using, wait for 30 minutes to meld flavors and firm up. Keeps well in the refrigerator for at least a week.

MAYO NOTES

Let refrigerated mayonnaise sit at room temperature for 10 to 15 minutes to soften and awaken. It will be tastier in banh mi.

If the plunger (pusher) of your food processor has a tiny hole, leave the plunger in the feed tube and just pour the oil into the plunger to automatically dispense the oil into the mayonnaise.

To remove the chill from the egg, crack it into a bowl and let sit for 15 to 20 minutes.

For blender mayonnaise, put all the ingredients *except* the oil in the blender jar. Put on the lid and replace the center cap (plug) with a funnel. On medium speed, whirl the ingredients until creamy (up to 60 seconds for the cilantro Maggi mayo), then slowly add oil through the funnel as directed in the recipe.

To soften stiff mayonnaise, mix in water by the teaspoon. Thicken by adding oil by the tablespoon. Enrich mayonnaise with an extra egg yolk during the initial blending.

To rescue "broken" mayonnaise, put 1½ tablespoons of just-boiled (very very hot) water into a bowl. Whisk in 1 to 2 tablespoons of the broken mayonnaise until smooth. Continue whisking in the remaining mayonnaise, 1 to 2 tablespoons at a time, until fully incorporated. If the result is too light tasting, let cool for about 5 minutes, then whisk in oil by the tablespoon to thicken. Cover and chill for 2 hours to firm up before using.

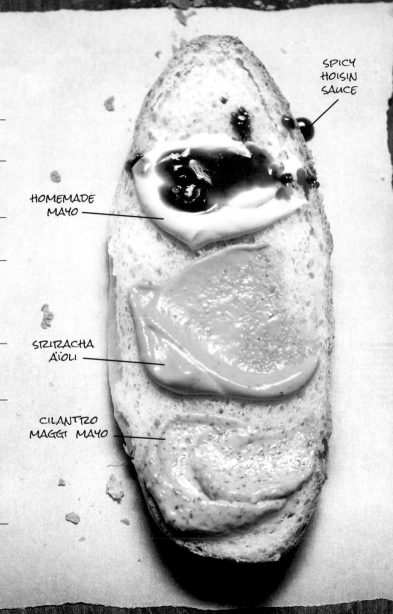

SPICY HOISIN SAUCE

HOMEMADE MAYO

SRIRACHA AÏOLI

CILANTRO MAGGI MAYO

sriracha aïoli

Makes 1¼ cups (300 ml) · **Takes about 5 minutes, plus 30 minutes resting**

Yes, you can squirt Sriracha sauce directly into a banh mi, but why not take a more voluptuous approach? Work the chile sauce into the mayonnaise emulsion—stirring Sriracha into premade mayo yields an off taste and thin texture. Use robust American-made Rooster brand Sriracha or nuanced Thai-made Shark or Sriraja Panich brands, sold at Asian grocers. Use a measuring cup with a spout for pouring the oil; for a blender method and other helpful hints, see Mayo Notes on page 25. Tester Thien-Kieu Lam enjoyed this aïoli in banh mi and as a dip for tiny boiled potatoes.

1 medium clove garlic, minced and mashed or put through a press

¼ teaspoon salt

1 tablespoon distilled white vinegar

3 tablespoons Sriracha chile sauce

1 large egg, near or at room temperature

1 cup (240 ml) canola oil

Put the garlic, salt, vinegar, Sriracha, and egg into the food processor's work bowl. Start the processor and, after a creamy orange mixture forms, 5 to 10 seconds, pour the oil through the feed tube in a slow, steady stream as thin as angel hair pasta. Midway through, after things thicken, pour a thicker stream, as wide as spaghetti.

After about 2 minutes, all the oil should be incorporated. Your mayonnaise should be creamy and spreadable; the Rooster brand yields a thicker result than the Thai brands (if it's curdled or soupy—broken—see Mayo Notes on page 25).

Taste the mayonnaise and if needed, pulse in extra salt for savoriness, vinegar for tartness, and Sriracha for heat. Transfer to an airtight container. Before using, wait for 30 minutes to intensify flavors and firm up. Keeps well in the refrigerator for at least a week.

NOTE

Because of the heat in this aïoli, use fewer chile slices (or omit them) in your sandwich.

raw egg yolks

How safe are raw eggs? Fairly safe: it's estimated that just 1 in 20,000 raw eggs in the U.S. is contaminated with salmonella. To minimize risk, I don't eat raw eggs often, and I buy good fresh eggs with clean, intact shells. If you prefer, you can find pasteurization instructions on the Internet, or try eggless mayo (page 28).

cilantro maggi mayonnaise

Makes 1¹/₃ cups (330 ml) · **Takes about 10 minutes, plus 30 minutes resting**

This happy green mayo distills Maggi Seasoning sauce's unique savoriness and balances it with a playful fruitiness. It's a brilliant condiment created by Diep Tran, the Vietnamese-American chef and owner of Good Girl Dinette in Los Angeles. To ensure a clean cilantro flavor, wash and pat the herb dry with paper towels. Employ a measuring cup with a spout for pouring the oil; when preparing this in a blender (see Mayo Notes, page 25), make the creamy mixture, then put the funnel in place, and add the oil.

A handful of cilantro sprigs (1 oz / 30 g total), coarsely chopped

1 tablespoon chopped shallot

½ small serrano or jalapeño chile, seeded and chopped

1 large or extra-large egg yolk, near or at room temperature

1 tablespoon fresh lemon juice

1½ tablespoons Maggi Seasoning sauce

1 cup plus 2 tablespoons (270 ml) canola oil

Using a food processor, mince the cilantro, shallot, and chile, pausing to scrape down the sides as needed. Add the egg yolk, lemon juice, and about half of the Maggi. Run the machine for 60 seconds to create a creamy, green-speckled mixture.

With the machine running, start pouring the oil through the feed tube in a slow, steady stream as thin as angel hair pasta. About halfway through, when an emulsion has formed, pour a thicker stream as wide as spaghetti.

After about 2 minutes, all the oil should be incorporated, and the mayo will be soft and spoonable (if it's curdled or soupy—broken—see Mayo Notes on page 25). Finish by whirling in the remaining Maggi. Taste and, if needed, blend in extra lemon juice or Maggi. Transfer to an airtight container. Before using, wait for 30 minutes to develop flavors and firm up. Store refrigerated for at least a week.

NOTES

Unless you enjoy lots of cilantro and Maggi, go light on (or omit) them in your sandwich when this mayo is involved.

Use the leftover egg white in herbed salmon cakes (page 79) or, as tester Alyce Gershenson suggests, substitute it for one of the whole eggs in the chicken katsu and tilapia recipes (pages 68 and 75).

eggless mayonnaise

Makes about 1¼ cups (300 ml) · **Takes about 15 minutes, plus 1 hour of resting**

This mayonnaise is for folks who follow a vegan or low-fat diet, as well as curious cooks. It's remarkably tasty and spreadable, lighter than regular mayonnaise. The keys to this recipe are draining silken tofu for a creamy texture, employing xanthan gum to bind and thicken, and masking the soy flavor. Powdery, buff-colored xanthan gum is sold at natural foods and specialty markets; to buy a small amount, check the bulk foods section. Select either a custardy, soft silken tofu or a denser water-packed block; Azumaya and Wildwood brands work well.

7 to 8 ounces (210 to 240 g) silken tofu

¼ plus ⅛ teaspoon salt

1 small clove garlic, minced and mashed or put through a garlic press

2 teaspoons Dijon mustard

2 teaspoons fresh lemon juice or distilled white vinegar

¼ plus ⅛ teaspoon xanthan gum, plus more as needed

6 tablespoons (90 ml) canola or other neutral-flavored oil

Cut the tofu into ¾-inch (2-cm) chunks and set on a super thick layer of paper towels (I fold an extra large one to make 6 layers). To drain, set aside for 5 minutes if using water packed silken tofu, or 10 minutes if using custardy tofu. You should net around 7¼ ounces (220 g).

Blot excess moisture from the tofu, then transfer to the bowl of a food processor or the jar of a blender. Add the salt, garlic, mustard, and lemon juice (or vinegar). Whisk together the xanthan gum and oil, then add to the processor; you don't have to stream it in like regular mayo. Run the machine for about 30 seconds, or until a thick, creamy mixture forms. You should be able to plop it from a knife. If it's runny, blend in 1 or 2 extra pinches of xanthan gum. The mayonnaise firms up and the flavor intensifies during resting. Adjust the flavor as needed with salt, mustard, lemon juice, or vinegar. Transfer to a jar then let sit for an hour before using; refrigerate for up to a week. If it separates slightly, stir it up.

VARIATIONS

For a **vegan Sriracha aïoli**, whirl the drained tofu and oil-and-xanthan gum mixture with the salt, garlic, vinegar, and 2 tablespoons of Sriracha sauce.

To make an **eggless Maggi cilantro mayonnaise**, puree the following in the processor: 1 ounce (30 g) coarsely chopped cilantro sprigs, 1 tablespoon chopped shallot, ½ small serrano or jalapeño chile that's been seeded and chopped up, 1 tablespoon fresh lemon juice, 1½ tablespoons Maggi Seasoning sauce, and the oil-and-xanthan gum mixture. Scrape down the sides, then add the drained tofu and blend to a creamy, thick consistency.

garlic yogurt sauce

Makes about 1 cup (240 ml) · **Takes about 5 minutes, plus 1 hour or more to mature**

I originally made this tangy, creamy sauce for a Viet take on Turkish-German doner kebab (page 95) and ended up using it like tartar sauce on seafood sandwiches. It's incredibly versatile and flexible. Use a large garlic clove if you enjoy its strength. Add dried or fresh herbs for earthiness. A rich-tasting low-fat Greek yogurt, like Fage brand, yields terrific results.

1 clove garlic, minced and mashed or put through a press

Scant ¼ teaspoon sugar

Scant ¼ teaspoon salt

⅓ cup (90 ml) mayonnaise, homemade (page 24) or store bought

⅔ cup (150 ml) low-fat Greek yogurt

Optional additions: generous 1 teaspoon dried mint or oregano, or 2 to 3 tablespoons finely chopped dill fronds or mint leaves

In a bowl, stir together all the ingredients to combine well. Cover and set aside at room temperature for an hour to develop flavor, or refrigerate for up to 2 days. Taste and adjust the flavor with salt or sugar before using. Enjoy slightly chilled or at room temperature.

NOTE

A spoon is best for spreading the sauce onto bread. I usually don't add Maggi or soy sauce with this sauce because they aren't totally copacetic. Sprinkle some coarse salt, such as kosher, into your sandwich if you want an extra savory note.

mock maggi sauce

Makes about ¹/₂ cup (120 ml) · **Takes 5 minutes, plus 25 minutes for cooling**

If you can't find Maggi Seasoning sauce (page 7) or need a gluten-free alternative, make a close knockoff using Bragg Liquid Aminos. The health food–era seasoning is close to Maggi's flavor and available at many natural foods markets and some supermarkets; sweeten and reduce it a bit, and it works as a straight substitute for Maggi.

½ cup (120 ml) Bragg Liquid Aminos

1 tablespoon sugar

In a butter warmer or similarly small saucepan, bring the liquid aminos and sugar to a boil. When the surface is covered with bubbly action, remove from the heat. Let cool and concentrate for 20 to 25 minutes before using.

Store in a small bottle or jar. Keep in the cupboard for about 2 weeks or refrigerate for longer.

making banh mi to go

When preparing banh mi to go, keep the sandwich as dry as possible. Crisp the bread and line it with mayo, Maggi, and the main filling. Put the pickle in one zip-top plastic bag and the cucumber, chile, and cilantro in another. Wrap the sandwich in parchment paper and use a rubber band to hold things together. Finish assembling right before you eat.

spicy hoisin sauce

Makes 1 cup (240 ml) · **Takes 5 minutes**

By combining and doctoring up two favorite Asian sauces you get an absurdly tasty result. This simple condiment has a wonderful junk-food quality—garlicky, spicy, salty, sweet, and viscous—but doesn't seem so bad because you mixed it up yourself! I got the idea from Charlie Hong Kong, an Asian-fusion fast food joint in Santa Cruz (my hometown). This sauce is good in sandwiches featuring grilled meats and fried foods, such as the chicken katsu banh mi on page 68.

6 tablespoons (90 ml)
Thai sweet chile sauce

¼ cup (60 ml) hoisin sauce

2 tablespoons unseasoned
rice vinegar

2 tablespoons regular
soy sauce

Whisk together all the ingredients in a bowl. Taste and, if needed, fine-tune with additional vinegar to offset the sweetness of the chile sauce. Aim for a tangy-sweet-salty flavor. Refrigerate for up to a month.

NOTES

Instead of Maggi or soy sauce, spoon this onto the bread after laying down the mayo. You can also offer the sauce on the side for guests to add to their sandwiches as they eat.

For extra heat, tester Laura McCarthy's teenage son suggested a few hearty squirts of Sriracha chile sauce.

daikon and carrot pickle

Makes about 3 cups (750 ml) · **Takes about 20 minutes, plus 1 hour for marinating**

If you only have one pickle for banh mi, this is it. Many banh mi shops opt to use only (or mostly) carrot for their *do chua* (literally "tart stuff"). In your kitchen, emphasize the slight radish funk for a sandwich with more character and cut the vegetables big enough to showcase their crunch; limp pickles get lost. Select daikon that's firm, relatively smooth, and no wider than 2 inches (5 cm). A batch of this pickle requires one that's about the length of a forearm. See Notes for worthy daikon substitutes.

1 medium daikon, about
1 pound (450 g)

1 large carrot, about
6 ounces (180 g)

1 teaspoon salt, fine sea salt
preferred

2 teaspoons plus ½ cup
(3.5 oz / 105 g) sugar

1¼ cups (300 ml) distilled
white vinegar

1 cup (240 ml) lukewarm
water

Peel and cut the daikon into sticks about 3 inches (7.5 cm) long and ¼ inch (6 mm) thick, the width of an average chopstick. Peel and cut the carrot to match the size of the daikon sticks but slightly skinnier. Put the vegetables in a bowl. Toss with the salt and 2 teaspoons of the sugar. Massage and knead the vegetables for 3 minutes, or until you can bend a piece of daikon and the tips touch without breaking. They will have lost about a quarter of their original volume.

Flush with running water, then drain in a mesh strainer or colander. Press or shake to expel excess water. Transfer to a 4-cup (1 l) jar.

For the brine, stir together the remaining ½ cup (105 g) sugar with the vinegar and water until dissolved. Pour into the jar to cover well. Discard any excess brine. Use after 1 hour or refrigerate for up to a month.

NOTES

If the daikon gets stinky, open the jar and let it air out for 15 minutes before using. The pickle hasn't gone bad.

When daikon is unavailable, try another radish or similar kind of vegetable, such as red radishes, watermelon radishes (red meat radish), and purple top turnips. Pickles made with watermelon and red radishes are a striking pink-orange. The turnip will be stark white.

Whatever you select, it should have bite. I usually choose red radishes a good 1 inch (2.5 cm) wide, and turnips and watermelon radishes weighing about 8 ounces (225 g) each. If using watermelon radishes or turnips, peel then cut them into sticks like you would the daikon. Treat the carrot as suggested in the main recipe.

Leave red radishes unpeeled and cut them into rounds a generous 1/8 inch (8 mm) thick. Cut the carrot lengthwise, then thinly cut the halves on the bias. The shapes won't match, but carrot rounds take longer to pickle. After tossing the vegetables in salt and sugar, let them sit for about 10 minutes so they'll be easier to squeeze. Brine as usual.

citrusy red cabbage pickle

Makes about 3 cups (750 ml) ▪ **Takes about 20 minutes, plus 1 day aging**

Some modern banh mi include a cabbage slaw, but it can be lacking. To ensure plenty of tangy goodness and crunch, I pickle the cabbage. For fragrant, thin peel, gently scrub your citrus then use a vegetable peeler to obtain the strips.

3½ cups packed (12 oz / 350 g) shredded red cabbage

1¼ teaspoons salt, fine sea salt preferred

¼ cup firmly packed (2 oz / 60 g) light or dark brown sugar

⅔ cup (150 ml) water

¾ cup (180 ml) distilled white vinegar

2 strips lemon or lime peel, each about the width and length of your smallest finger

Put the cabbage into a 4-cup (1 l) jar, packing it in as needed. In a saucepan, bring the salt, sugar, water, and vinegar to a boil, stirring to dissolve the solids. Remove from the heat, wait for the bubbling to subside, then pour into the jar. Tuck in the citrus peel. As the cabbage softens, use a spoon to push it down to immerse it all in brine.

Leave at room temperature, uncovered, to wilt the cabbage and cool. It's ready to use once cooled, but will develop more of a citrus edge if capped and refrigerated overnight. Store in the fridge for up to 2 months.

NOTES

Briefly drain what you need in a mesh strainer before putting it into banh mi. If the peel comes out with the cabbage shreds, put it back in.

Substitute other kinds of citrus peel, such as orange and tangerine, to vary the flavor, or add a couple of cloves to the brine. You can refresh the pickle with new strips of peel.

As you use up the cabbage, repurpose the brine for salad dressing. I like to use it for a **raw kale salad** by massaging the hand-torn greens with several spoonfuls of the brine along with salt and pepper to taste. After the kale softens, I add a whisper of grapeseed oil.

tweaking the flavor of pickles

After a pickle has matured, taste and, if needed, fine-tune things with extra vinegar or sugar. Let it sit for 1 or 2 days, retaste, and note your changes for future batches.

GREEN TOMATO AND
LEMONGRASS

SNOW PEA AND
LEMONGRASS

RED RADISH
AND
CARROT

SHALLOT

CITRUSY
RED CABBAGE

DAIKON AND CARROT

pickled shallot

Makes about 2 cups (500 ml) · **Takes about 15 minutes, plus 1 day aging**

Vietnamese banh mi makers sometimes add raw green or yellow onion to cut the fattiness in rich and/or meaty sandwiches. I prefer a slightly sweet pickled shallot that is blushing pink and mild tasting, safe and charming enough for a banh mi snack date.

Viet shallots are traditionally pickled whole and take about a week to mature. For this quicker version, I cut the shallots first. Select shallots that feel firm and heavy for their size. When they are not available or pricey, use red onion. The texture and flavor won't be as bright, but the magenta color will be gorgeous. I keep jars of both in my fridge.

8 ounces (225 g) large shallots, or 1 medium red onion

½ teaspoon salt, fine sea salt preferred

Scant 6 tablespoons (2.5 oz / 75 g) sugar

⅓ cup (80 ml) water

⅔ cup (150 ml) distilled white vinegar

Cut off the stem and root ends of each shallot. Halve them lengthwise, then peel off the skin and any dry-looking layers to reveal a smooth, glossy surface. Cut each half lengthwise to yield wedges, about ⅓ inch (1 cm) at the widest part. To reduce harshness, put the shallot in a bowl with water to cover for 5 to 10 minutes. Drain well, then pack into a 2-cup (500 ml) jar. Do your best to fit it all in.

Combine the salt, sugar, water, and vinegar in a small saucepan. Bring to a boil, then remove from the heat. Once the boiling subsides, pour the brine into the jar. Gently push the shallot down with chopsticks or a spoon to submerge. Let sit, uncovered, until totally cooled.

Though the shallot can be eaten once cooled, it will mellow and taste better if capped and left to mature overnight in the refrigerator. Keep refrigerated for as long as a month.

NOTES

Terrific in a sandwich featuring Vietnamese cold cuts (pages 40 to 52). It's also a handsome and tasty garnish for crostini topped with sardines in tomato sauce (page 76). In a full-size banh mi, mix the shallot pickle with another pickle because the shallot alone can overwhelm.

For a quick and refreshing pickled shallot and arugula or watercress salad, in a bowl, combine ½ cup (120 ml) of pickled shallot with 1 tablespoon of the pickling brine and 2 pinches of salt, 2 pinches of pepper, and about 1½ teaspoons of canola oil. Add 2 handfuls of arugula or tender stems and leaves of watercress and toss. Taste and adjust the seasonings to flatter the greens and shallot. Serve as a side or stuff in banh mi instead of the vegetables.

snow pea and lemongrass pickle

Makes 2 cups (500 ml) · **Takes about 25 minutes, plus 1 day aging**

Despite looking delicate, snow peas keep their integral flavor when pickled. Their crispness is perfect in banh mi and as a side nibble. Leftover brine is good for making salad dressing. See the Variation for a green tomato version.

8 ounces (225 g) snow peas

1 medium lemongrass stalk

1 small clove garlic, lightly crushed

Generous ¼ teaspoon dried red pepper flakes, or 1 fresh Thai or serrano chile, split lengthwise

Pinch of ground turmeric

¼ plus ⅛ teaspoon salt, fine sea salt preferred

¼ cup (1.75 oz / 50 g) sugar

½ cup (120 ml) plus 1 tablespoon distilled white vinegar

½ cup (120 ml) water

Snap the ends off each snow pea, peeling and discarding the stringy fiber. Pack the peas into a 2- to 3-cup (500 to 750 ml) glass jar. Set aside.

Trim the lemongrass (see sidebar). Cut two 3- to 4-inch (7.5 to 10 cm) pieces, then smack them with the back of a heavy knife or a meat tenderizer to break the fibers and release flavor; save or discard the remaining stalk.

Put the lemongrass in a small saucepan. Add the garlic, red pepper flakes, turmeric, salt, sugar, vinegar, and water. Bring to a boil, take off the heat, and wait for the bubbling to subside. Pour over the snow peas. Use a spoon or spatula to gently push the peas, lemongrass, and chile down. Aim to submerge them in the brine.

Let cool completely, partially covered, at room temperature. Cap and refrigerate overnight before eating. Keep for up to a month.

NOTE

If the snow peas are no bigger than an index finger, slide them whole into banh mi. Large ones can be cut lengthwise or crosswise into smaller, manageable pieces. Eat the chile, if you like, but not the lemongrass.

VARIATION

To turn this recipe into a fabulous green tomato pickle, use ⅔ pound (300 g) unripened, green tomatoes. Choose hard fruits. Keep them whole or halve or quarter them. Cut crosswise into pieces about ¼ inch (6 mm) thick. Omit the turmeric from the brine, if you like. It's a South-meets-Southeast Asia pickle.

trimming lemongrass

Chop off the tough bottom base with its hard core and the green, woody top section. Peel away loose or dry outer layers to reveal a smooth, tight stalk. The trimmed, usable section will be 4 to 8 inches (10 to 20 cm) long, depending on the size of the original stalk. Prep as directed in the recipe; if you have to chop lemongrass, whack trimmed pieces with a meat tenderizer or the spine of a cleaver to break the fibers and make cutting easier. Freeze trimmed lemongrass in a zip-top bag for up to 3 months; it retains most of its flavor and is easier to chop than fresh.

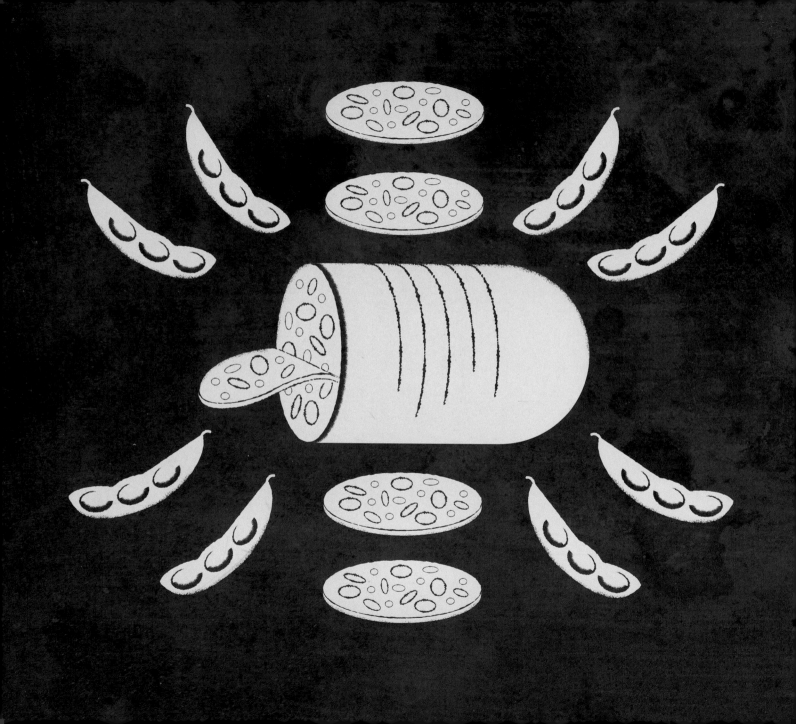

cold cuts

Step inside a Viet deli, bakery, or market and you're sure to see various cold cuts—sausages, headcheese, and pâté, for example. They are a core part of Vietnamese cooking: premade flavorful proteins that last a long time. And they're a natural for sandwiches. If you keep one or two of these cold cuts and spreads—some of which are vegetarian—in the fridge, you'll be able to make banh mi with minimal effort.

garlic pepper pork tenderloin

Makes about 1 pound (450 g) · **Takes 45 minutes, plus 2 hours cooling**

While my sister Tasha attended Harvard Law School, she dearly missed Viet food and often hand carried *thit banh mi o*, a garlicky cold cut, on her travels from California to Cambridge. My mother made it by boiling a highly spiced mixture of boneless pork stuffed inside a casing of pork skin. The quintessential Viet sandwich meat cured Tasha's homesickness.

You don't need a doting mom (or to be a hardcore cook) for your banh mi fix. Use pork tenderloin. Its cylindrical shape and ham-like texture mimic the traditional version well. Simply season and boil the pork. *Thit banh mi o* usually has a pinkish rind from red food coloring. When I added colorant for authenticity, the result bordered on gruesome. Don't do it.

1 pork tenderloin, about 1⅓ pounds (600 g)

½ brimming teaspoon black peppercorns

2 cloves garlic, coarsely chopped

¼ teaspoon Chinese five-spice powder

½ teaspoon sugar

1¼ teaspoons salt, fine sea salt preferred

Pat the pork dry with paper towels, then cut in half crosswise into 2 shorter pieces. Tear or cut 2 parchment paper rectangles, each about 8 by 12 inches (20 by 30 cm). Ready 2 pieces of aluminum foil, each about the size of a small baking sheet (12 by 16 inches / 30 by 40 cm). Set the foil pieces on your work surface, narrower sides close to you, then center a piece of parchment on top of each. Fill a 3- or 4-quart (3 or 4 l) pot two-thirds full of water. Bring to a boil over high heat, cover, then lower the heat to keep hot.

Toast the peppercorns in a small dry skillet or saucepan over medium heat for a few minutes, until fragrant. Cool briefly, then use a mortar and pestle to pound to a cracked texture. Add the garlic, five-spice powder, sugar, and salt. Mash and pound to a rough paste.

Smear and rub the seasoning paste onto the meat. Roll each piece of pork in parchment paper, folding down the ends to enclose. Then roll each in a piece of aluminum foil, closing the ends well to form a chubby sausage shape. Use kitchen twine to securely tie together (see page 43).

Return the pot of water to a boil, then drop in the pork. After the water returns to a boil, maintain the boil for 30 minutes. Retrieve and cool to room temperature before eating. (Chill overnight for the best flavor.)

Before making sandwiches, thinly slice the pork into rounds and coat it in the juices for extra flavor.

NOTES

Enjoy this pork tenderloin in a special **combination banh mi** (see page 52) for varied textures and flavors, or feature it on its own.

Refrigerate wrapped or unwrapped with the juices in a plastic zip-top bag or airtight container for up to 5 days.

GARLIC PEPPER
PORK TENDERLOIN

CHEATER'S SILKY SAUSAGE

cheater's silky sausage

Makes 2 sausages, 10 ounces (300 g) each ▪ **Takes about 45 minutes, plus 2 hours cooling**

What are those pale thin slices of savoriness in your *dac biet* special combo sandwich? It's *gio lua* (or *cha lua*), a super popular banh mi cold cut that's often called "pork roll" or "Vietnamese ham." Typically made from pork, but sometimes chicken too, it's the Viet equivalent of bologna (mortadella). This is a streamlined version of the recipe from my book *Into the Vietnamese Kitchen*. It's also the basis for the two recipes that follow.

Seasonings

1½ teaspoons sugar

1½ teaspoons baking powder

1 tablespoon tapioca starch

1½ tablespoons canola oil

2½ tablespoons fish sauce

2 or 3 tablespoons water (use lesser amount for ground chicken)

1 pound (450 g) ground chicken thigh or ground pork (about 85 percent lean)

2 pieces fresh or thawed banana leaves, each about 6 by 10 inches (15 by 25 cm), trimmed of brown edges, rinsed, and wiped dry (see Notes for substitutes)

Fill a 3- or 4-quart (3 or 4 l) pot two-thirds full of water. Bring to a boil over high heat, lower the heat, then cover to keep hot.

Put all the seasonings and the water into the bowl of a food processor. Pulse several times to blend. Drop in the meat as large chunks. Run the machine until the ingredients gather into a rough ball. Let sit for 3 to 5 minutes to hydrate and season the meat.

Meanwhile, put 2 pieces of aluminum foil, each about the size of a small baking sheet (12 by 16 inches / 30 by 40 cm), on your work surface, narrower sides close to you. Center the leaves, smoother side up, atop the foil. Set aside.

When the meat is done resting, grind the mixture in the processor for about 2 minutes to achieve a relatively smooth, light pink paste. Pause to scrape the sides as needed. Visible flecks of meat are fine.

Use a spatula to plop half of the paste near the lower edge of a banana leaf. Pat and neaten up the paste into a fat log; dip the spatula in water if things are too sticky. Roll up the leaf to encase the paste. Then roll the green cylinder up in the foil. Fold the ends closed and tap them down to set the shape. Tie with kitchen twine to keep secure during cooking (see opposite). Repeat to make the other sausage.

Return the pot to a boil. Drop in the sausages. After the boil returns, cook for 25 minutes. Expect the foil to darken and the sausages to swell and float. Retrieve with tongs, then cool completely or chill (it's easier to cut) before slicing into thin rounds; discard the banana leaf before tucking into sandwiches.

NOTES

Make an old school banh mi with this sausage, butter, salt, and lots of black pepper, or add other cold cuts and the fixings for a classic **combination banh mi** (see page 52).

Store in an airtight container or zip-top bag, wrapped or unwrapped, for up to a week, or freeze for up to 2 months.

How fatty is your ground pork? In general, the paler the pork, the more fat it contains. Regular ground pork at mainstream butcher counters are about 85 percent lean, the equivalent of "Grade A" at Chinese and Viet markets. Ask your butcher for clarification, then eyeball the pork. For ground chicken thigh, head to a butcher counter at a natural foods market or specialty grocer. Or grind your own pork or chicken (page 45).

Banana leaf is sold at many Chinese, Southeast Asian, and Latin markets. To substitute, cut unbleached parchment paper to size. Or use 2 large chard leaves. Trim the leaves' spines out, then blanch the green halves in the pot of water. Arrange each pair slightly overlapping to encase the paste. Serve the sausage slices with the edible chard intact, as pictured on page 41.

Tapioca starch (tapioca flour) is sold at Asian grocers and health food markets. You can substitute 2 teaspoons cornstarch, but the texture will be slightly firmer, a hair off the ideal.

tying tips

1. Loop 1 yard (1 m) of twine around the sausage about 1 inch (2.5 cm) from one of the edges, crossing the twine to secure.

2. Pull the twine around the length of the sausage, crossing it in the back about 1 inch (2.5 cm) from the other edge. Loop one end of twine around the sausage to secure; the sausage naturally turns.

3. Finish with a knot. The sausage is ready for cooking.

garlicky silky sausage

Makes 2 sausages, 10 ounces (300 g) each ▪ **Takes about 45 minutes, plus 2 hours cooling**

Many silky sausages sold at Vietnamese markets contain garlic and black pepper. They may be labeled as *gio lua* but they are technically *gio Hue*, a punchy rendition from the central Vietnamese city known for both gutsy flavors and delicate imperial cuisine. Here's how to make the tasty cold cut from the master cheater's silky sausage recipe on page 42.

Seasonings

1 clove garlic, minced and mashed or put through a press

½ rounded teaspoon black peppercorns, toasted in a skillet until fragrant, then pounded with a mortar and pestle to a coarse texture

1½ teaspoons sugar

1½ teaspoons baking powder

1 tablespoon tapioca starch

1½ tablespoons canola oil

2½ tablespoons fish sauce

2 or 3 tablespoons water (use lesser amount for ground chicken)

1 pound (450 g) ground chicken thigh or ground pork (about 85 percent lean)

2 pieces fresh or thawed banana leaves, each about 6 by 10 inches (15 by 25 cm), trimmed of brown edges, rinsed, and wiped dry (for substitutes see page 43)

Follow the cheater's silky sausage recipe on page 42 to make this sausage. Ready a pot of water to boil the sausages. Meanwhile, use a food processor to transform the seasonings, water, and meat into a paste.

Wrap the paste up in banana leaf and foil to form 2 sausages and tie each with kitchen twine to secure (see page 43). Boil the sausages for 25 minutes, then cool before using or storing.

NOTE

No mortar and pestle for pounding peppercorns? Pulse them in a spice grinder or put them in a heavy skillet, then crush with a small, heavy saucepan.

beef and dill sausage

Makes 2 sausages, 10 ounces (300 g) each ▪ **Takes about 45 minutes, plus 2 hours cooling**

Less common than pork or chicken *gio lua* but equally delicious is beefy *gio bo*, flecked with dill and spiked with pepper. Super lean meat is usually used but I've found that ground chuck or 85 percent lean ground beef works well. Because beef is traditionally a luxury meat in Vietnam, this sausage is a special treat. This recipe refers back to the cheater's silky sausage recipe on page 42.

Seasonings

½ rounded teaspoon black peppercorns, toasted until fragrant, then pounded with a mortar and pestle to a coarse texture

1½ teaspoons sugar

1½ teaspoons baking powder

1 tablespoon tapioca starch

1½ tablespoons canola oil

2½ tablespoons fish sauce

3 tablespoons chopped fresh dill fronds

4½ tablespoons (70 ml) water

1 pound (450 g) ground chuck or 85 percent lean ground beef

2 pieces fresh or thawed banana leaves, each about 6 by 10 inches (15 by 25 cm), trimmed of brown edges, rinsed, and wiped dry (for substitutes see page 43)

Follow the cheater's silky sausage recipe on page 42 to make this sausage. Ready a pot of water to boil the sausages. Meanwhile, use a food processor to transform the seasonings, water, and meat into a paste.

Wrap the paste up in banana leaf and foil to form 2 sausages and tie each with kitchen twine to secure (see page 43). Boil the sausages for 25 minutes, then cool before using or storing.

grinding meat in a food processor

Choose boneless meat with about 15 percent fat, such as beef chuck, pork shoulder, and chicken thighs. Trim the gristle but keep the fat. Cut the meat into thumbnail-size chunks. To avoid mushy results, freeze the meat, food processor blade, and bowl for 30 minutes. Work in small batches, such as 6 ounces (180 g) for an average processor. Pulse to chop and grind, pausing every 10 to 15 pulses to check the texture, scraping down as needed.

gateway chicken liver pâté

Makes 1¼ cups (10 oz / 300 g) · **Takes 30 minutes**

Fragrant and deeply savory, liver pâté anchors many traditional banh mi. When I don't have time to make and age an old-fashioned loaf of *pa-te gan*, I fall back on this velvety alternative. Prepared in small batches with delicate chicken livers and leftover bread innards from past banh mi forays, the result is mild, and good enough to lick off the spreader.

8 ounces (225 g) chicken livers, yellowish membranes removed (use fingers or a knife tip)

One 14.5-ounce (410 g) can low-sodium chicken broth, or 2 cups (480 ml) lightly salted chicken stock

1 bay leaf

8 black peppercorns

1 ounce (30 g) bread, trimmed of crust

3 tablespoons (45 g) unsalted butter

½ cup (2 oz / 60 g) chopped shallot

2 cloves garlic, coarsely chopped

1 tablespoon cognac or brandy

¼ teaspoon black pepper

Rounded ¼ teaspoon salt, fine sea salt preferred

¼ plus ⅛ teaspoon Chinese five-spice powder

½ teaspoon fish sauce (optional, for umami goodness)

Put the livers, broth, bay leaf, and peppercorns in a small saucepan. Bring to a simmer over medium-high heat, then lower the heat to around medium-low to poach for 6 to 8 minutes, until just cooked through. A little pinkness in the center is fine.

Use chopsticks or a fork to transfer the livers to a food processor. Strain the cooking liquid through a fine-mesh strainer, discarding scummy bits. Add ⅓ cup (90 ml) of the liquid to the processor, reserving the rest. Tear the bread into chunks, dropping them into the processor.

Melt the butter in a medium skillet over medium-high heat. Add the shallot. Let sizzle and fry, stirring often, for 4 minutes, or until starting to turn golden. Slide to a cool burner, dump in the garlic and cognac, stir, and let sit until the hissing subsides.

Transfer to the food processor. Add the pepper, salt, five-spice powder, and fish sauce. Puree, pausing to scrape down the sides. Keeping in mind that the pâté firms up during resting, taste and add extra cooking liquid to soften, bread to stiffen or mellow the liveryness, and seasoning to pop flavors. Transfer to a container and let mellow for 10 minutes before using, or refrigerate for up to 1 week.

NOTES

Enjoy as a simple, old-fashioned banh mi lined with salted butter, a layer of pâté, and a sprinkling of salt and black pepper. Or make a combo, such as the *dac biet* (page 52).

The best livers come from the tastiest birds; head to good butcher shops to find them, or freeze them yourself when you cook whole chickens. To ensure even poaching time, select livers of similar size. The leftover cooking liquid can be used to cook soup or rice. In a pinch, sub chopped liver from a deli, or make a quick version from liverwurst (see opposite).

quick pork liver pâté

Makes scant 1¼ cups (9 oz / 270 g) · **Takes 30 minutes**

If you enjoy pork liver's earthiness, line your banh mi with this pâté. It's got an edge and funk that advanced offal eaters will appreciate. (The chicken liver version, opposite, is a lovely freshman-level pâté.) There's no need to source fresh pork liver from specialty grocers or ethnic markets. Simply buy liverwurst, such as Wellshire or Farmer John brands, then doctor it up.

8 ounces (225 g) liverwurst

3 tablespoons (45 g) unsalted butter

½ cup (2 oz / 60 g) chopped shallot

2 cloves garlic, coarsely chopped

1 tablespoon cognac or brandy

Chinese five-spice powder

Black pepper

Fine sea salt or fish sauce

Cut the liverwurst into large chunks and let it sit out for at least 15 minutes to remove some of the refrigerator chill.

Meanwhile, melt the butter in a medium skillet over medium-high heat. Add the shallot. Let sizzle and fry, stirring often, for 4 minutes, or until starting to turn golden. Slide to a cool burner, dump in the garlic and cognac, stir, and let sit until the sizzling subsides.

Transfer the shallot mixture to a food processor and finely chop. Add the liverwurst, then puree. As needed, soften the result with a tablespoon or so of water. Season with about ⅛ teaspoon of each: five-spice powder, black pepper, and sea salt or fish sauce. The amount you use depends on your taste and the liverwurst. Let sit for 10 minutes to develop the flavor before readjusting the flavor and making sandwiches. Refrigerate in an airtight container for up to 1 week.

NOTES

Feature alone or with other fillings in a *dac biet* combo (page 52). Any of the pâtés in this chapter are great as banh mi crostini (page 10) or simply with crackers.

Some mild-tasting braunschweigers (such as Oscar Mayer) can stand in for liverwurst.

To mellow over-livery pâté, mix in a bit of mayo before spreading it on bread.

nuke that pâté!

To enjoy pâté at full bloom, make sure it is at room temperature and spreadable. If it's cold and/or firm, gently revive it via the microwave's defrost function. Blasts lasting 15 to 20 seconds remove the chill and soften the pâté.

edamame pâté

Makes 1⅓ cups (11 oz / 330 g) ▪ **Takes 30 minutes**

To add earthy richness to a sandwich without going the livery route, try this upbeat green edamame pâté. I developed it for meatless banh mi and discovered that it's good with chicken and seafood, too.

1⅓ cups (8 oz / 225 g) frozen shelled edamame

2 tablespoons canola oil

⅓ cup (1.5 oz / 45 g) chopped shallot

1 large clove garlic, chopped

¼ plus ⅛ teaspoon salt, fine sea salt preferred

¼ plus ⅛ teaspoon curry powder

1 teaspoon sugar

½ cup (120 ml) water

1 green onion, white and green parts, chopped

If the edamame is still frozen when you get working, put into a strainer and flush with hot water to quickly thaw. Set aside to drain.

In a small saucepan, heat the oil over medium-high heat. Add the shallot and cook, stirring, for 3 to 4 minutes, or until starting to turn golden. Add the garlic and let sizzle for 30 seconds, until fragrant.

Add the edamame, salt, curry powder, sugar, and water. Bring to a vigorous simmer, cover, then lower the heat to maintain the simmer. Cook for 5 minutes, checking occasionally, or until half of the water is gone. Uncover and stir in the green onion. Once it wilts, remove from the heat. Cool for 5 to 10 minutes.

Transfer to a food processor and whirl until relatively smooth and spreadable, occasionally pausing to scrape down the sides. Add water and salt, if needed, to adjust the texture and seasoning. Let flavors bloom for 10 minutes before using. Refrigerate in an airtight container for up to 5 days.

NOTES

Spread atop mayonnaise and drizzle on the Maggi for punch before adding other sandwich elements.

Instead of curry powder, try a pinch or two of ground turmeric with garam masala or Chinese five-spice powder.

GATEWAY CHICKEN LIVER PÂTÉ

EDAMAME PÂTÉ

DAC BIET
SPECIAL COMBO

headcheese terrine

Makes 1²/₃ pounds (750 g) ▪ **Takes about 2¹/₂ hours, plus 1 day aging**

A classic Viet cold cut, headcheese imparts a slight crunch to banh mi. Vietnamese headcheese is dense and firm, not gelatinous and soft like its Western counterpart. I love old-school *gio thu* and have molded it the traditional way, in a recycled food can lined with banana leaf. For a modern, less fussy approach, I make a terrine using only ears and shoulder. The rich, gelatinous stock flavored with cilantro helps glue the mixture together, yielding a handsome stained glass effect.

2 medium pig ears (12 oz / 350 g total)

1 pound (450 g) relatively lean boneless pork shoulder or pork sirloin

2 teaspoons salt, fine sea salt preferred

1 rounded teaspoon black peppercorns

1 small yellow onion, halved

A handful of cilantro sprigs (1 oz / 30 g total)

½ teaspoon black pepper

1 tablespoon fish sauce

Hold the ears over a flame to singe off stray hairs, rinsing afterward. Quarter each ear into triangular and squarish pieces. Cut the pork shoulder into thick pieces, like chunky decks of cards. Put the ears and shoulder into a 4-quart (4 l) pot. Add 8 cups (2 l) water. Bring to a boil, skim off the scum, then add the salt, peppercorns, onion, and cilantro. Maintain a rolling boil for 45 minutes. Remove from the heat. Let sit uncovered for 45 minutes to cool and finish cooking.

Meanwhile, select a 4-cup (1 l) rectangular glass food container or loaf pan to hold the terrine. Line the bottom and two sides with parchment paper or banana leaf, letting it extend above the edge by 1 inch (2.5 cm).

Remove the ears and pork shoulder from the pot. Strain the cooking liquid through a fine-mesh strainer; skim off the fat if there's too much. Pour 2 cups (480 ml) of the liquid into a saucepan (save leftover liquid for soup or sauces). Bring to a boil and cook to reduce it by about a third, 6 to 12 minutes. Set aside to cool.

Cut the ears into strips as wide as a woman's pinkie finger. Cut the pork shoulder into thick forefinger-size pieces. Put into in a medium nonstick skillet and cook over medium heat for 10 to 16 minutes, stirring gently, until things stick together, signaling the release of gelatin. Lower the heat slightly if there's too much browning. Expect pops and hisses near the end.

Sprinkle in the pepper and fish sauce, stirring to distribute well. Gently cook for 3 minutes, or until the mixture is tacky again. Remove from the heat. Cool for a few minutes, then spoon the mixture into the mold, firmly packing it down as you work.

Make sure the reduced cooking liquid is *not* hot before pouring into the mold to nearly cover the solids; you won't use all the liquid. Cover with parchment or banana leaf. To evenly distribute pressure, place a piece of Styrofoam tray (cut to size) or a smaller storage container lid on top. Finish with a 2 to 3-pound (1 to 1.5 kg) weight, enough to force the liquid to rise and cover the solids. Refrigerate until set, about 3 hours, then remove the weight, cover, and age overnight. To unmold, run a knife around the edge, then lift the terrine out by the parchment paper or leaf. Discard the leaf or paper. With the rougher side down, thinly slice for sandwiches.

continued

NOTES

Although you can let the headcheese fly solo in banh mi, it's most often used for a tour de force combo, as described below.

Fresh or thawed pig ears can be found at Chinese, Viet, and Mexican markets; portable butane lighters work well to singe hairs. A butcher shop that practices a head-to-tail rigor will have excellent ones. Thick pork shoulder or sirloin steaks work well. Just debone them.

To store, refrigerate in the mold for a week or freeze portions for up to 2 months.

Aside from banh mi, eat the terrine with hot rice (the gelatin melts to coat the grains) or serve it with mustard and dark bread. You'll have plenty.

invent your own banh mi!

What kind of sandwiches can you make with the cold cuts from this chapter? A lot, and that's the beauty of make-ahead cold cuts. Keep one, two, or three kinds around and a banh mi is easily within reach. Viet sandwiches can feature a single protein or combine a couple or several. Feel free to pair cold cuts with other recipes in this book; try liver pâté and Chinese barbecued pork (page 89) or one of the following.

One-Meat Wonder Plain and simple, like a good ham sandwich. Just the bread, meat, salt and pepper and maybe some fat. Make this if you want to taste the meat. Old-timers, purists, and kids enjoy these, which are good as breakfast banh mi. To make: Line the bread with butter or mayo. Lay in the meat and finish with salt and pepper.

One-Meat Saigon One meat plus the fixings: mayo, vegetables, and chile. This style of sandwich began in early 1940s Saigon, where it was generically called *banh mi thit nguoi* (cold cut sandwich). To make: Follow the master banh mi sandwich recipe on page 9 using one protein from this chapter. Any pickle or mayo works, though the daikon and carrot pickle and homemade mayo are classic.

Two-Meat Pairing A fancied-up banh mi for when you want to present contrasting flavors and textures without going overboard with too many meats. Rich and earthy pâté is often one of the proteins used, but variations are endless. To make: Follow the master banh mi sandwich recipe on page 9 and use two meats from this chapter. Adorn with pickles, etc. or omit the veggies for a two-meat wonder.

Three- or Four-Meat Special (Dac Biet) The Viet version of a hoagie, filled with multiple meats and the whole shebang of accouterments. At banh mi shops, "the *dac biet*" may be translated as the "special" or "classic" sandwich (pictured on page 50). To make: Line the bread with mayo and shots of Maggi. From the bottom up, smear on liver pâté, then add slices of: headcheese terrine (page 51), any silky sausage (pages 42, 44, and 45), and/or garlic pepper pork tenderloin (page 40). Use daikon and carrot pickle, cucumber, chile, and cilantro.

Vegetarian (Banh Mi Chay) Soy-centric, meatless sandwiches made just like regular banh mi. The baked Maggi tofu (page 53) or edamame pâté (page 48) are great alone or together. Add the fixings to make your sandwich sparkle.

baked maggi tofu

Makes 14 ounces (420 g) · **Takes 45 minutes, plus time to press and marinate**

Can you turn tofu into a vegetarian cold cut suitable for sandwiches? Yes, you can. Just apply the Chinese method of making seasoned pressed tofu: simmer and marinate super-firm tofu with Maggi and black pepper, and garlic for earthiness. See the lemongrass Sriracha tempeh (page 112) for a similar recipe.

1 pound (450 g) super-firm tofu

3 cups (720 ml) water

4 cloves garlic, smashed

1 teaspoon black pepper

1 teaspoon packed dark brown sugar

1½ to 2 tablespoons Maggi Seasoning sauce or mock Maggi sauce (page 30)

1 tablespoon canola oil

Cut the tofu into slices like decks of playing cards, each about ⅝ inch (1.5 cm) thick. To expel excess moisture, use 2 baking sheets. Lay a non-terry dishtowel (or paper towels) on one of the sheets and arrange the tofu slices on top, then another towel, then the other baking sheet. Finish with a 4-pound (2-kg) weight, such as two large cans of tomatoes. Set aside at room temperature for 2 to 4 hours, until the tofu feels slightly moist—you shouldn't fear it falling apart when you wiggle it.

In a medium saucepan, combine the water, garlic, pepper, sugar, and enough Maggi for a mild savoriness. Put the tofu in the pan in two layers; they should be covered by liquid. Bring to a simmer over medium-high heat. Lower the heat to medium or medium-low and gently simmer for 15 to 20 minutes to allow the tofu to absorb the seasonings. Set aside, uncovered, to completely cool. If the tofu isn't covered by liquid, transfer to a container where it will be; otherwise, keep in the pan. Cover and marinate in the refrigerator for 8 hours or overnight.

Remove the tofu from the marinade and discard the marinade. Lean the tofu up against the rim of a plate to drain for about 15 minutes. Meanwhile, position a rack in the middle of the oven and preheat to 450°F (230°C / gas mark 8). Line a baking sheet with parchment paper. Right before baking, put the oil on a small plate. Coat each piece in the oil, putting it on the baking sheet as you work.

Bake for 10 to 12 minutes, until the pieces are gently sizzling and have darkened at the edges. Use a spatula to turn each piece over. Bake for another 5 minutes to further brown. Remove from the oven and let rest for about 10 minutes before transferring to a rack to finish cooling completely. Expect the tofu to firm up, dry, and darken. Thinly cut it at a steep angle to create nice wide pieces for sandwiches.

NOTES

The tofu is great with the edamame pâté (page 48) in a banh mi. Or let it play the starring role.

Keep in an airtight container in the fridge for up to 2 weeks.

Super-firm tofu is often sold in vacuum-sealed packages; there's little visible water.

chicken

The definitive chicken sandwich of my youth wasn't stuffed with chicken salad bound by mayonnaise. It was baguette filled with garlicky roast chicken imbued with the flavors of Maggi Seasoning sauce. We made them at home and bought them at Little Saigon sandwich shops in Westminster, California. Happy as I was with that rendition, I've stayed open to new opportunities to make chicken-centric banh mi, like the ones in this chapter.

hanoi grilled chicken

Makes enough for 6 banh mi · **Takes 1 hour**

Brilliant foods are often simple foods. I had this tangy-salty grilled chicken at a Hanoi cafe in 2003 and was struck by its bright flavor. So much so that I replicated it upon returning to the States. It's great with rice but is perfectly at home stuffed into baguette. When possible, grill it over an open flame for a nice charred flavor. The heavy dose of black pepper lends an edge to this chicken.

1½ pounds (675 g) boneless, skinless chicken thighs

¼ teaspoon sugar

Brimming ¼ teaspoon salt

1¼ teaspoons black pepper

1 tablespoon fish sauce

1 tablespoon fresh lime juice

About 1½ tablespoons canola oil

Trim and discard big fat pads from the chicken thighs. If the thighs are large and/or super uneven in thickness, butterfly them (see page 58). Set aside.

In a bowl, stir together the sugar, salt, pepper, fish sauce, and lime juice. If needed, tweak the flavor to get a slightly tart-sweet, salty finish. Add the oil, then the chicken, coating the pieces well. Cover with plastic wrap and marinate at room temperature for 30 minutes.

To grill the chicken, preheat a gas grill to medium or prepare a medium-hot fire, or use a stove-top grill pan heated over medium-high heat with a little oil brushed on. Cook the chicken for 6 to 10 minutes, turning several times, until clear juices flow out when you pierce the flesh with the tip of a knife. Cool for 10 minutes before cutting across the grain. Tumble in the cooking juices to include extra flavor in the sandwich.

NOTE

For a **Hanoi grilled chicken banh mi**, use any of the accouterments. Keep leftovers for up to 3 days, warming the chicken in the microwave oven or skillet over medium heat, adding any cooking juices for depth.

when to flip the chicken

After putting a chicken thigh on a hot grill or pan, let it sear undisturbed. When there is an opaque border of about ¼ inch (6 mm), flip the chicken. It should release easily and have nice browning on the underside. The second side will cook in less time, and you can turn it as you like.

classic chicken

Makes enough for 6 banh mi ▪ Takes 1 hour

I grew up eating my mother's old-school version of this garlicky chicken. Bone-in and oven-roasted, our French-influenced *ga ro-ti* (roast chicken) was flavored by Maggi Seasoning sauce, a colonial import. We regularly had the chicken for dinner and saved leftovers to make banh mi. Nowadays, when I make the chicken specifically for sandwiches, I simplify things by using boneless thighs (my favorite part) and cooking on the stove top; to grill, see the Hanoi chicken recipe on page 57.

1½ pounds (675 g) boneless, skinless chicken thighs

2 cloves garlic, minced and mashed or put through a press

¼ teaspoon black pepper

½ teaspoon sugar

About 1 tablespoon Maggi Seasoning sauce, mock Maggi sauce (page 30), or regular soy sauce

1 teaspoon dark soy sauce, or ¾ teaspoon regular soy sauce and ¼ teaspoon molasses

About 1½ tablespoons canola oil

Trim and discard big fat pads from the chicken thighs. If the thighs are large and/or super uneven in thickness, butterfly them (see sidebar). Set aside.

Combine the garlic, pepper, sugar, Maggi, and soy sauce in a bowl. Taste and adjust the seasonings to create an intense salty-sweet flavor. When satisfied, add the oil. Stir to combine, then add the chicken, coating the pieces well. Cover with plastic wrap and marinate at room temperature for 30 minutes.

To cook the chicken, use a stove-top grill pan or nonstick skillet. Heat it over medium-high heat with a little oil to coat. Cook the chicken for 8 to 10 minutes, flipping midway. The chicken is done when clear juices flow out when you pierce the flesh with the tip of a knife.

Cool for 10 minutes before cutting across the grain. Coat in cooking juice to flavor further, then make sandwiches.

NOTES

For a **classic chicken banh mi**, pair the sliced chicken with homemade mayonnaise (page 24), Maggi, daikon and carrot pickle (page 33), chile, cucumber, and cilantro. To go nouveau, try it with any of the mayos, pickles, and condiments.

Refrigerate leftovers for up to 3 days. Refresh with any cooking juices in a microwave or skillet over medium heat.

how to butterfly chicken thighs

Lay the thigh smooth side down on your cutting board. Wielding your knife horizontally, slash the big mound of flesh to create a flap of meat. Stop just shy of cutting all the way through. Fold back the meat flap that you just created. The thigh should now be about 50 percent longer and relatively even in thickness. If the result seems awkwardly large, cut it crosswise into two smaller, squarish pieces.

chicken sausage patties

Makes 12 patties, for 6 banh mi · Takes 45 minutes

Viet cooks love to season ground meat and grill it up to enjoy with rice noodles, lettuce, and herbs, or to tuck into sandwiches. I like to combine rich-tasting ground chicken thighs with lots of green onion, garlic, and a touch of chile. The flour lightly binds. This mixture is very soft, so you'll form and immediately cook the patties in two batches. For ground dark meat chicken, head to a natural foods market or specialty grocer. If it's not already in the case, ask the butcher. Or grind it yourself (see page 45).

2 cloves garlic, minced and mashed or put through a press

⅔ cup (2 oz / 60 g) finely chopped green onion, green and white parts

1 Thai or serrano chile, minced, seeds optional

¼ teaspoon sugar

1 tablespoon fish sauce

2½ tablespoons oyster sauce

1½ tablespoons all-purpose flour, rice flour (brown or white), or almond meal flour

1½ pounds (675 g) ground chicken thigh

1 to 2 tablespoons canola oil

In a bowl, combine the garlic, green onion, chile, sugar, fish sauce, and oyster sauce. Taste and adjust to get a pleasant salty-sweetness with a little heat. Stir in the flour, then mix in the chicken. Divide into 12 portions. Set near the stove with a bowl of water.

Heat a large nonstick skillet over medium-high heat before adding 2 to 3 teaspoons of oil. Wet your hands, then form a 3-inch (7.5-cm) patty; if you like, make oblong ones to match the shape of a banh mi roll. Pass it between your hands a few times to smooth out the surface, then gently lay it on the skillet. Repeat to make 5 more.

Cook for 3 to 4 minutes per side, until nicely browned and no longer pink in the center (pierce with a knife tip to test). Add extra oil, then form and cook 6 more patties. Let rest for a few minutes before using.

For regular banh mi, slice the patties to evenly distribute the meat across the bread; angle your knife to make broad pieces. Keep them whole for sliders (page 10).

NOTES

Craft a tasty **chicken sausage banh mi** with plain or cilantro Maggi mayonnaise (page 27), spicy hoisin sauce (page 31), daikon and carrot pickle (page 33), cucumber, and cilantro. You may not need the fresh chile heat.

The sausage mixture can be made a day ahead. Let it sit at room temperature for about 30 minutes to remove the chill.

chicken sate

Makes enough for 6 banh mi · **Takes 1 hour**

Taking a cue from Bryant Ng, the sandwich-loving chef/owner of noteworthy Los Angeles restaurants such as The Spice Table, I grill Malaysian chicken sate and slide the meat off the skewer into baguette for banh mi. The result is stunning.

1½ pounds (675 g) boneless, skinless chicken thighs

2 teaspoons whole coriander seeds or ground coriander

2 teaspoons whole fennel seeds or ground fennel

¾ teaspoon salt

1 teaspoon ground turmeric

2 tablespoons packed dark brown sugar or shaved dark palm sugar

2 cloves garlic, coarsely chopped

2 tablespoons coarsely chopped ginger

1 fat stalk lemongrass, trimmed and coarsely chopped (⅓ cup / 35g; see page 37)

½ cup (2.25 oz / 65 g) coarsely chopped shallot

1 tablespoon canola oil, plus more as needed

As needed, butterfly the chicken (see page 58 for details) to even out the thickness. Cut across the grain into strips about 1 inch (2.5 cm) wide. Put into a bowl and set aside.

If starting with whole coriander and fennel seeds, toast them in a skillet over medium heat until fragrant, about 3 minutes. Cool, then grind to a sawdust-like texture in a spice grinder. Put the spices into a mini or full-size food processor and add the salt, turmeric, sugar, garlic, ginger, lemongrass, shallot, and oil. Process into a wet paste, pausing and scraping to ensure an even texture. Add to the chicken and use your hands to massage and coat well.

Thread the chicken onto skewers, covering most of each skewer. (With 10-inch / 25-cm bamboo skewers, you'll fill 4 or 5 of them. If you plan to cook them on the stove top, use short skewers or cut long ones to fit the grill pan.) Give each loaded skewer a gentle squeeze to ensure that the chicken hugs the skewer (this keeps it succulent). Set on a plate, cover, and marinate at room temperature for 30 minutes.

To grill the chicken, preheat a gas grill to medium-hot, prepare a medium-hot charcoal fire, or use a stove-top grill pan heated over medium-high heat with a little oil brushed on. Right before grilling, brush oil on the skewers. Cook for about 12 minutes, turning frequently and basting with oil, until the chicken is slightly charred and done. Nick a piece to check. Briefly cool before sliding the chicken off the skewers.

NOTE

For **chicken sate banh mi**, combine the chicken with plain or flavored mayo and red cabbage pickle (pages 27 and 34) along with the chile, cucumber, and cilantro. As pictured here, it's also great with the green tomato and lemongrass pickle and, if you like, pickled shallot too (pages 36 and 37).

sri lankan black curry chicken

Makes enough for 6 sandwiches · Takes about 1¹/₂ hours

When Viet people eat curry with baguette, they typically dip the bread into the spiced coconut-scented sauce. San Francisco chef Alex Ong sent me his recipe for this bewitching curry (the name comes from the dark-colored spice blend), insisting that it would be perfect *stuffed inside* a baguette for banh mi.

He was right, but to avoid a soggy sandwich, I hand shredded the cooked chicken and recooked it in the sauce, allowing it to fry in the residual oil and become encrusted with the seasonings. It became like an Indonesian rendang or, as my husband put it, a curried chicken carnitas. It's fantastic.

⅛ teaspoon ground cardamom

¼ teaspoon black pepper

½ teaspoon ground cinnamon

¾ teaspoon ground mace or nutmeg

1 teaspoon ground clove

1 teaspoon ground cumin

1½ teaspoons ground coriander

3 cloves garlic, coarsely chopped

A hefty ¾-inch (2-cm) knob of ginger, peeled and coarsely chopped

1 slender stalk of lemongrass, trimmed and coarsely chopped (2 to 3 tablespoons; see page 37)

1 large Fresno or jalapeño chile, coarsely chopped

¾ cup (3.5 oz / 115 g) coarsely chopped shallot

1¾ pounds (800 g) boneless, skinless chicken thighs

2 tablespoons virgin coconut or canola oil

1 teaspoon brown mustard seeds

¾ teaspoon salt

1⅓ cups (330 ml) coconut milk

In a small bowl, combine the cardamom, pepper, cinnamon, mace, clove, cumin, and coriander. Set the spice blend near the stove. Use a mini or full-size food processor to finely chop the garlic, ginger, lemongrass, chile, and shallot. Keep by the spices. Trim the chicken of large fat pads and set nearby.

In a 4-quart (4 l) pot, heat the oil over high heat. When hot enough to sizzle a mustard seed upon contact, add all of them. Swirl or stir for about 10 seconds, until a few seeds crackle and pop, then add the shallot mixture. Cook for 3 to 5 minutes, stirring, until no longer raw smelling.

Lower the heat slightly, add the spice blend, and stir for about 30 seconds, until toasty and a dark chocolate color. Add the chicken, turning to coat with seasonings. Add the salt and coconut milk, which should barely cover the chicken; add water if necessary. Adjust the heat to simmer, uncovered, for 30 minutes. Stir occasionally to prevent scorching; the pot contents will shrink to roughly half the original volume. Remove from the heat and let cool for 20 minutes.

Transfer the chicken to a plate and hand shred, with the grain, into pinkie finger–wide pieces; set aside. Pour the sauce into a large nonstick skillet. Over high heat, vigorously simmer for about 6 minutes, stirring frequently, until reduced by half and pools of coconut oil dot the

continued

surface. Lower the heat slightly, then add the chicken and any accumulated sauce. Cook, stirring frequently, for 8 to 12 minutes, until the chicken has darkened to a rich brown and is coated with crusty seasoning; the sauce will no longer be visible and the chicken will gently fry in hissing oil.

Cool slightly, then season with extra salt, if needed. For great flavor, enjoy the chicken slightly above room temperature in banh mi.

NOTES

To let the rich, spiced chicken shine in a **black curry chicken banh mi**, use just a bit of regular mayo and omit or go light on Maggi. Select any of the pickles, or combine one with the pickled shallot (page 36). Remember the chile, cucumber, and cilantro. Try as a regular banh mi, slider, or steamed-bun banh mi (pages 10 and 117).

Refrigerate for up to 3 days, reheating in a microwave oven or a skillet over medium heat, with a splash of water to moisten and refresh. Perfect for make-ahead banh mi.

Instead of fresh chile, add ½ to ¾ teaspoon of cayenne to the spice blend. Or substitute 2 tablespoons of a favorite curry powder for the spice blend.

If you have fresh curry leaf (*Murraya koenigii*), fry 5 or 6 large leaves along with the mustard seeds; remove the leaves before reducing the sauce.

rotisserie chicken and cracklings

Makes enough for 6 banh mi · **Takes about 15 minutes**

With a rotisserie chicken in hand, you can make banh mi in a snap. At the market, select a rotisserie chicken that's been minimally seasoned (sometimes labeled "plain"), then doctor up the meat with salt and lots of black pepper. If you like, turn the skin into crisp cracklings.

A small (about 2 lb / 1 kg) rotisserie chicken

Salt, kosher preferred

Black pepper

Splash of canola oil

Use your fingers and/or a knife to take the meat off the bone, reserving the skin for cracklings, if you like. Save any juices. Tear the meat into pieces the size of your index finger so you can tuck it into the bread. You'll have about 1¼ pounds (565 g). Mix with the reserved juices and set aside. If you are not making cracklings, skip this next step.

Crackling lovers—cut the pieces of skin into strips the length and width of your index finger (they'll shrink down). Put into a skillet and cook over medium heat, stirring occasionally, for about 6 minutes, until the skin has rendered fat and is the color of an autumn leaf. Transfer to a paper towel to drain and sprinkle lightly with salt. Reuse the skillet (with fat still in it) to reheat the chicken.

Before using the chicken for sandwiches, season it with salt and lots of pepper; aim for a savory flavor in the flesh. Gently reheat the chicken in a skillet over medium heat with a couple splashes of oil or the fat left over from making cracklings. Use a handful of the soft, slightly warm chicken along with some cracklings for each sandwich.

NOTES

For **rotisserie chicken and cracklings banh mi**, use any of the mayos or the garlic yogurt sauce (page 29), Maggi, snow pea pickle (page 37), cucumber, and cilantro. Sprinkle on the cracklings after laying down the seasoned chicken. Add fresh chile if desired.

Instead of salt, use Maggi, mock Maggi sauce (page 30), soy sauce, or tamari to season the chicken. Sauté 2 minced cloves of garlic in the oil before adding the chicken. Feel free to use leftover roast chicken or turkey.

crispy drunken chicken

Makes enough for 5 or 6 sandwiches ▪ **Takes 45 minutes**

Named one of America's best new sandwiches in 2011 on *Huffington Post*, the crispy drunken chicken banh mi created by Seattle-based chefs Eric and Sophie Banh is like a Chinese-Vietnamese chicken nugget sandwich—fried chicken chunks cloaked in a tangy earthy sauce.

    What makes the chicken "drunk"? Rice wine, Eric revealed; it cuts the chicken flavor and allows other flavors to pop. In my rendition, lots of cornstarch seals in moisture and aids crisping. See Notes to source Chinkiang vinegar and Shaoxing rice wine, or use the (worthy) supermarket substitutes.

1¼ pounds (565 g) boneless, skinless chicken thighs

Rounded ¼ teaspoon salt

3 tablespoons plus ⅔ cup (3 oz / 90 g) cornstarch

1 teaspoon plus 2 tablespoons regular soy sauce

3½ tablespoons Shaoxing rice wine or dry sherry

1 tablespoon canola oil plus more for deep-frying

3 cloves garlic, smashed

A 1-inch (2.5-cm) section of unpeeled ginger, sliced and smashed with the flat side of a knife blade

3 tablespoons sugar

3 tablespoons Chinkiang vinegar, or 1½ tablespoons balsamic and 1½ tablespoons cider vinegar

6 tablespoons water

2 teaspoons cornstarch dissolved in 2 tablespoons water

Trim and discard big fat pads from the chicken thighs. If the thighs are large and/or super uneven in thickness, butterfly them (see page 58). Cut the chicken into nuggets, each a good 1½ inches (3.75 cm). In a bowl, combine the salt, 3 tablespoons cornstarch, 1 teaspoon soy sauce, 2 tablespoons of the rice wine, and 1 tablespoon oil. Add the chicken, stirring to coat well. Set aside to marinate for 15 minutes.

Meanwhile, in a 1-quart (1 l) saucepan, combine the remaining 2 tablespoons soy sauce and 1½ tablespoons rice wine with the garlic, ginger, sugar, vinegar(s), and water. Taste and tweak for a tart-sweet-savory flavor; expect a smoky edge from Chinkiang vinegar. Bring to a simmer over medium heat, then slightly lower the heat to percolate for 1 to 2 minutes, until you smell the garlic and ginger essence. Stir in the cornstarch slurry. Increase the heat slightly, and when nearly boiling and thick, about 45 seconds, remove from the heat. Cool for 5 minutes, then strain; discard the solids. Set aside, uncovered, to further cool and concentrate. You should net a very generous ¾ cup (180 ml).

To deep-fry, use a wok or deep skillet. Pour in oil to a depth of 1 inch (2.5 cm), then bring to about 350°F (180° or 175°C) over high heat. Clip on a deep-fry thermometer to gauge oil temperature, or stick a dry chopstick into the hot oil: if bubbles rise immediately to the surface, the oil is ready.

As the oil heats, dredge the chicken in the remaining ⅔ cup (90 g) cornstarch, knocking off excess. In batches, fry the chicken for 2 to 3 minutes, turning often, until crispy and the color of golden autumn leaves. Drain on a rack. Return the oil to temperature between batches.

Put the warm chicken in a bowl and coat with as much sauce as you like; I save a bit for serving on the side or lining the bread. Make banh mi immediately, while the chicken retains a delicate crispness.

NOTES

Given the sauce's bold flavor, you may not need Maggi or soy sauce in a **crispy drunken chicken banh mi**. Use any of the mayonnaises, and skip the pickle if the sauce is tart enough for you. If there's leftover sauce, serve it on the side or drizzle it on the mayo. Tuck in ribbons of romaine or iceberg lettuce instead of cucumber, which can be unwieldy alongside the chicken chunks. Include chile and lots of cilantro.

At a Chinese market, shop for Pagoda brand Shaoxing rice wine and Gold Plum brand Chinkiang vinegar. Both are reliable.

Fry the chicken several hours in advance and reheat on a baking sheet in a regular oven or toaster oven preheated to 450°F (230°C / gas mark 8) for about 8 minutes, until sizzling and recrisped; flip midway if not using a rack. For a lighter version, make the oven-fried chicken katsu on page 68 but dress it up with this sauce instead of the spicy hoisin sauce.

human flesh–sandwich girl

With so many accent marks involved, Vietnamese language is a tough one to master. For example, *bánh mì thịt nguội* refers to a Saigon-style cold cut sandwich that includes mayonnaise, pickles, cucumber, cilantro, and chile. It's the definitive banh mi for many people.

When I was about twelve, I was tasked with writing our family's Little Saigon shopping list. On one occasion, my Mom told me to include banh mi. Instead of noting down *bánh mì thịt nguội*, I wrote *bánh mì thịt người*. When my parents read my list, they busted out laughing. I'd spelled human flesh sandwich. They loved my mistake (Viet people enjoy word plays) and told their friends, one of whom took to calling me the Human Flesh–Sandwich Girl. It pays to spell check and proofread.

For this book, we decided to omit the accent marks for typographical reasons but made an exception here to highlight the nuanced humor of Vietnamese language.

oven-fried chicken katsu

Makes enough for 6 banh mi · Takes about 30 minutes

I love to deep-fry but realize that many people are tortured by the thought of it. That's the reason behind this easy and flavorful recipe, a Viet take on popular Japanese fried pork cutlet sandwiches called *katsu sando*. The crispy egg-and-panko-coated chicken cutlets are great warm as well as cold, perfect for picnics and lunchboxes. They're a hit with children, testers Maki Tsuzuki and Thien-Kim Lam reported.

2 cups (4 oz / 120 g) panko breadcrumbs

1¼ pounds (565 g) boneless, skinless chicken breasts (each about 10 oz / 300 g)

Salt

Black pepper

2 large eggs

¼ cup (60 ml) canola oil

About ½ cup (2.5 oz / 75 g) all-purpose flour

In a large skillet over medium-high heat, toast the panko for 4 to 6 minutes until golden brown, like well-toasted coconut; dial in the color now as the panko darkens very little later. Stir frequently, lowering the heat as needed. Remove from the heat and let cool in the skillet, or transfer to a large plate to prevent overbrowning.

Position a rack in the upper third of the oven and preheat to 475°F (245°C / gas mark 9). Put a rack on a baking sheet and set aside.

Cut the chicken into pieces. First remove the long, slender breast tenderloins, if they're still attached; set aside. If the breast is huge (larger than your hand), cut it crosswise. With the smooth, curved side up, cut each piece of chicken breast horizontally into slices about ⅓ inch (8 mm) thick; hold the knife at a 20- to 30-degree angle to cut on the bias, which makes for more tender results. Use a meat tenderizer or saucepan to lightly pound each piece between two pieces of waxed paper or plastic wrap to a thickness of about ¼ inch (6 mm)—think scaloppini. Season with salt and lavish on the pepper.

In a bowl, beat the eggs, oil, and ½ teaspoon of salt. Set aside. Dredge the chicken in the flour (use a bowl or plastic bag), knocking off excess. Dip each piece of chicken in the egg, letting excess drip off, then coat in the toasted panko, pressing gently. Arrange as a single layer on the prepared baking sheet. Bake for 8 to 10 minutes, until faintly hissing, with patches of visible bubbles on the surface. Cool for about 5 minutes before removing from the rack. Cut the chicken to match the size and shape of the bread, then make sandwiches.

NOTES

Build a **chicken katsu banh mi** with regular mayonnaise, spicy hoisin sauce (page 31), red cabbage pickle (page 34), cucumber, and cilantro. Add fresh chile for extra heat.

Recrisp and warm leftovers in a preheated 375°F (190°C / gas mark 5) regular or toaster oven for about 4 minutes, flipping midway if not using a rack. Tester Laura McCarthy suggested turkey instead of chicken breast. See page 75 for a fish version.

seafood

Despite Vietnam's long coastline and innumerable seafood dishes, you don't come across many banh mi featuring fish, shellfish, or crustaceans. If a banh mi shop has a seafood option, it's likely to be made with the Viet equivalent of canned tuna: canned sardines in tomato sauce (page 76). There are local specialties, such as the fried fish cake sandwiches on Con Dao and Phu Quoc islands, according to Tracey Lister, author of *Vietnamese Street Food*.

But just because there are few traditional seafood-centric banh mi, you shouldn't refrain from crafting some yourself. Vietnamese cooking is open to creativity, and here are a few ideas from my kitchen to get you started.

shrimp in caramel sauce

Makes enough for 5 or 6 sandwiches · Takes about 30 minutes

Shrimp cooked in caramel sauce (*tom kho*) is among my favorite Viet comfort foods. I typically eat it with rice, but one day I slid leftovers into a roll for a surprisingly fantastic banh mi. Traditionally, *tom kho* is prepared with shell-on shrimp and caramel sauce, which is, basically, nearly burnt sugar. Most cooks lack a jar of caramel sauce in their pantry; here's a method for individual batches. Vigorously cooking shrimp for a long time seems counterintuitive, but it yields shrimp that seem almost candied.

1½ pounds (675 g) medium shell-on shrimp (35/40 count)

Salt

1 tablespoon fish sauce

½ medium yellow onion or 1 large shallot, thinly sliced

3 tablespoons sugar

2 or 3 drops distilled white vinegar or lemon or lime juice (optional, for preventing crystallization)

Generous 1 tablespoon canola oil

¼ to ½ teaspoon black pepper

1 green onion, green part only, cut into thin rings

Peel and devein the shrimp; put them in a colander and toss with ½ teaspoon of salt. Rinse, drain well, then put into a bowl. Add a big pinch of salt, then the fish sauce and onion. Set near the stove.

Select a heavy medium skillet or a shallow medium saucepan with a light-colored interior (to easily monitor the caramelization process). Put the sugar, 1 tablespoon of water, and the vinegar in the pan. Heat over medium heat, stirring with a metal spoon or rubber spatula, until relatively smooth and clear, about 1 minute. Stop stirring and let the sugar cook.

When the sugar is champagne yellow, after about 4 minutes, pay attention. Swirl the pan for about 1 minute to coax the sugar to a light tea color; swirl a bit longer for a darker shade and a slight bittersweetness. Faint smoke may rise toward the end.

Turn off the heat and let the sugar continue caramelizing on the hot burner until it is dark amber, about 3 minutes. Add a splash of water to the pan, then reheat over medium-high heat, stirring to loosen the caramelized sugar from the bottom. Add the shrimp and onion mixture, and raise the heat to high, so it is vigorously bubbling. Cook for 13 to 15 minutes, stirring frequently, until the shrimp are orange-brown and 1 to 2 tablespoons of slightly syrupy liquid remains.

Add the oil and cook for another minute; there will be little liquid left at the end. Off heat, stir in the black pepper and green onion. Taste and add a pinch of salt if you like. Enjoy warm or at room temperature in sandwiches.

NOTE

In a **shrimp in caramel sauce banh mi**, use the snow pea or daikon and carrot pickle (pages 37 and 33), cucumber, cilantro, and chile. Any of the mayonnaises will work. The shrimp flavor is bold, so you may not need Maggi.

viet oyster po' boy

Makes enough for 4 sandwiches · **Takes 30 minutes**

Banh mi and po' boy sandwiches share similar traits: French bread lined with mayonnaise and stuffed with pickles, raw veggies, and protein. Both are open to innovation. This riff on the Louisiana classic pays homage to the Viet fishing community in the Gulf Coast. The crisp, curry-flavored oysters make a dynamite banh mi. Jars or tubs of shucked oysters, sold at many supermarkets and Costco-type of retailers, work beautifully. For a Louisiana fish fry banh mi, tester Thien-Kim Lam suggests using catfish instead of oysters.

2 cups (16 fl oz / 480 ml) shucked oysters, small or medium preferred

About 1 teaspoon salt

1 teaspoon sugar

2 teaspoons curry powder

½ cup (2.5 oz / 75 g) all-purpose flour or corn flour (use the latter for extra crunch)

1 cup (5 oz / 150 g) regular or fine-grind cornmeal

1 teaspoon black pepper

1 large egg

½ cup (120 ml) milk or soy milk

Canola oil, for panfrying

Drain the oysters in a mesh strainer and give them a quick rinse. Set aside to drain. For the cornmeal coating, in a bowl, stir together ½ rounded teaspoon of the salt with the sugar, curry powder, flour, and cornmeal. In another bowl, whisk together the remaining ½ teaspoon salt with the pepper, egg, and milk. Set both near the stove, along with a plate and rack set on a baking sheet.

Pat the oysters well with paper towels to remove excess moisture. Working in 2 or 3 batches, dredge the oysters in the cornmeal mixture, knocking off excess. Dip each one in the egg wash, then replace it in the cornmeal. Recoat the oysters in cornmeal, then put them on the plate. (I often multitask by cooking one batch while prepping the next one.)

Heat a large skillet over medium-high or high heat. Add enough oil to film the bottom. If an oyster needs extra coating, do it right before laying it in the skillet. In batches, panfry the oysters for 2 to 3 minutes, turning frequently, until crisp on both sides. Cool cooked oysters on the rack. Wipe the skillet clean of cornmeal residue between batches and add more oil. Adjust the heat as needed.

When all oysters are fried, you can re-fry any that need extra crisping; if the coating falls off a few oysters due to hidden moisture, add the bits to your sandwich and move on. The oysters are good warm or at room temperature, as long as they still have crunch.

NOTES

Have all the sandwich fixings ready to go. Like with the fishwich, opposite, iceberg lettuce can replace the cucumber. Any of the mayonnaises (or the yogurt sauce) and pickles would be great. Maggi works for a salty hit because a **Viet oyster po' boy** can handle big flavors. The oysters are perfect for regular banh mi, sliders, and crostini (see page 10).

Corn flour (aka "superfine cornmeal") is employed for extra crunch. Instead of curry powder, try cayenne or paprika (smoked or regular); add enough so you can smell it in the coating mixture.

panko-crusted tilapia

Makes enough for 6 sandwiches · Takes about 30 minutes

While making the chicken katsu on page 68, I wondered how that nifty oven-frying method could be applied to create a fishwich with Viet flair. Several days of tinkering yielded these delicately crisp fillets accented by green onion, dill, and fish sauce—elements of Hanoi-style *cha ca*, a traditionally grilled fish eaten with rice noodles, lettuce, and herbs. Widely available tilapia is easy to handle, cooks up well with good flavor, and holds the crust nicely.

1¾ cups (3.75 oz / 120 g) panko breadcrumbs

2 tablespoons chopped dill fronds

2 tablespoons finely chopped green onion, green part only

6 small tilapia fillets (3 oz / 90 g each), or 3 medium-large tilapia fillets (6 oz / 180 g each)

Sea salt

Black pepper

2 large eggs

2 teaspoons fish sauce, or ½ teaspoon salt

¼ cup canola oil

About ⅓ cup (1.67 oz / 50 g) all-purpose flour

Position a rack in the upper third of the oven and preheat to 475°F (245°C / gas mark 9). Put a rack in a baking sheet and set aside. In a large skillet over medium-high heat, toast the panko for 4 to 6 minutes until golden brown, like well toasted-coconut; panko darkens very little during baking so set the color now. Stir frequently, lowering the heat if needed. Remove from the heat, cool a few minutes in the skillet, then add the dill and green onion.

If using small fillets, keep them whole. If using medium-large fillets, halve each lengthwise. Because of the fillet's natural contours, the halves will not be equal. To ensure no sandwich is cheated of fish, cut a thin piece off the dome-shaped top of the bigger piece and cook it, too (panko hides mistakes well, so don't worry about looks). Regardless, pat the fish dry with paper towels and season with salt and lots of pepper. Set aside.

In a bowl, beat together the eggs, fish sauce, and oil. Set aside. Dredge the fish in the flour (use a bowl or plastic bag), knocking off excess. Dip the fish in the egg, letting excess drip off, then coat in the panko mixture, pressing the panko into place.

Arrange the fish in a single layer on the rack in the baking sheet. Bake for 8 to 10 minutes, until faintly hissing; expect to see some tiny bubbles on the surface. Cool for 5 minutes before removing from the rack. These fillets are good warm or at room temperature as long as their crisp crust holds.

NOTES

For a terrific **Viet fishwich**, pair the fillets with any of the pickles (pages 33 to 37) but substitute delicate shreds of iceberg lettuce for the cucumber. Keep the chile and cilantro. Use any mayonnaise or the yogurt sauce to enrich the fish. Maggi peps things up.

Refresh and warm leftovers in a toaster oven preheated to 375°F (190°C) for about 4 minutes, flipping midway if not using a rack. Instead of tilapia, try catfish or snapper. Cut the fish into pieces about ⅓ inch (8 mm) thick, lest they cook up with soft spots underneath. Tester Jay Dietrich suggests adding lemon zest to the panko mixture.

sardine and tomato sauce

Makes enough for 12 to 16 crostini to serve 4 to 6, or 3 sandwiches · Takes about 15 minutes

An old-timey favorite, banh mi filled with sardines typically involves using the fish straight from the can. I prefer my grandmother's more flavorful approach: add fried shallot, doctor up the sauce, and warm the fish. The result is milder than tuna fish and just about as easy to put together.

A 15-ounce (420 g) can sardines in tomato sauce

½ teaspoon light or dark brown sugar

2 teaspoons fresh lime juice

1½ tablespoons ketchup

2 tablespoons canola oil

½ cup (2 oz / 60 g) chopped shallot

Drain the sardines, reserving 2 tablespoons of the tomato sauce in a small bowl. Use a fork to split open each sardine. If you like, lift off the spine bones; try to keep the fillets intact. Put on a plate and set aside.

To the reserved tomato sauce, add the sugar, lime juice, and ketchup. Set aside.

Heat the oil in a medium skillet over medium-high heat. Add the shallot and let sizzle and fry, stirring frequently, for about 4 minutes, until starting to turn golden.

Slide the skillet off the heat and wait for about 1 minute before adding the tomato sauce mixture (to avoid spattering). Give the mixture a stir, then arrange the fish in the skillet, skin side up.

Replace the skillet over medium heat, bring to a gentle simmer, then cook for about 2 minutes to blend the flavors; when done, the oil will have separated into little pools at the surface. Remove from the heat and cool briefly. Enjoy warm or near room temperature, while the fish remains slightly soft. Or refrigerate for up to 2 days and reheat in a skillet or microwave oven with a bit of water to moisten.

NOTES

Present **sardine banh mi** as appetizer-sized crostini (see page 10) or if you love the sustainable fish, pile them into a full-size sandwich. In full-size banh mi, add a fried egg or Thai fried omelet (page 111) to make the sardines go farther. The snow pea pickle (page 37) is the only one that doesn't work here.

Shop for the sardines at Chinese, Southeast Asian, and Mexican markets. At mainstream grocers, look in the canned fish or Latino foods sections. Ideal brands contain only sardines, tomato, and salt. Many older Viet expats consider Marock brand from Morocco to be their first choice.

canned french legacy

When the French occupied Vietnam, they introduced certain canned foods and brands that still linger in the Vietnamese culinary consciousness. That's why Vietnamese delis, bakeries, and markets carry canned sardines from Morocco, stout red cans of salty Bretel butter from France, and diminutive cans of liver pâté. Nostalgia aside, those foods are all quite decent tasting. Give them a try to savor a bit of colonial French Indochina.

NOTES

Make **herbed salmon cake banh mi** with the usual ingredients but substitute a leaf of soft lettuce for the cucumber. Try mint instead of cilantro or combine the two. The fish cakes are also terrific for lettuce wrap banh mi (page 120), with cucumber added for crunch.

Make ahead and refrigerate for up to 3 days or freeze for up to 1 month. Return to room temperature and revive in a skillet over medium-high heat with a splash of oil for about 2 minutes, turning frequently.

removing skin from a fish fillet

1. Cut the fillet crosswise into pieces roughly 3 inches (7.5 cm) wide. Set the fillet skin side down on the cutting board.

2. Run your finger along the thicker edge to separate the flesh from the skin and form a gap.

3. Slide a boning or fillet knife in the gap. Angle the blade downward to cut the skin away from the flesh.

4. When there's enough detached skin, hold it to keep the fillet in place. Saw and push the knife all the way through to the other edge to finish.

spicy wok-seared shrimp

Makes enough for 6 sandwiches ▪ **Takes about 20 minutes**

I wanted to make a grilled shrimp banh mi, but dealing with shrimp skewers proved tedious for sandwiches, and the flavor wasn't special. Instead, I coated the shrimp with cornstarch, then seared them at high heat, a method that sealed in moisture and let the surfaces brown as if the shrimp were grilled. A final toss with garlic, green onion, and chile further boosted flavor.

1½ pounds (675 g) medium shell-on shrimp (35/40 count)

¾ teaspoon salt

Brimming ½ teaspoon white pepper

1 teaspoon packed light or dark brown sugar

2½ teaspoons cornstarch or tapioca starch

2 tablespoons canola oil

3 cloves garlic, finely chopped

1 Fresno or jalapeño chile, quartered, then cut crosswise into narrow pieces (keep seeds intact)

2 green onions, white and green parts, cut into thick rings

Peel and devein the shrimp. To refresh, put them in a colander or mesh strainer and toss with ½ teaspoon of the salt. Rinse and drain well, then pat with paper towels to dry. Transfer to a bowl. Add the remaining ¼ teaspoon salt and the pepper, sugar, and cornstarch. Stir to coat the shrimp well. Set aside.

Heat a large wok or medium skillet over high heat. Add 1½ teaspoons of the oil, then half of the shrimp, spreading them out into one layer. Cook them undisturbed for 1 to 2 minutes, or until the tail tips turn bright orange. Use a spatula to flip and cook the other side for 1 to 2 minutes more, until done. Aim to sear one or both sides well. Let some edges pick up chocolate brown coloring, as if you grilled them. Transfer to a plate, add 1½ teaspoons of oil to the skillet, then repeat with the remaining shrimp.

When all the shrimp are cooked, lower the heat to medium-high, then add the remaining 1 tablespoon oil. Add the garlic, chile, and green onion. Cook for 15 to 30 seconds, until fragrant. Return all the shrimp and any juices to the wok, then cook to coat well and heat through, 1 minute. Transfer to a plate or bowl and cool slightly before assembling banh mi.

NOTE

Have the sandwich components for your **wok-seared shrimp banh mi** ready to go, as you want the shrimp on the warm side. If the chile heat in the shrimp isn't hot enough for you, add fresh chile slices and/or line the bread with Sriracha aïoli (page 26). The cilantro Maggi mayonnaise (page 27) lends good flavor and color contrast, as does the snow pea pickle (page 37), though any of the other pickles would work well.

fresh chile heat

When it's cold outside as they're growing, fresh chiles have less oomph, so add extra slices to your sandwiches; pull back in the summer months when their heat is on. Slices closer to the stem are hotter, as a chile's punch is mostly contained in the capsaicin glands (membranes) attached to the seeds.

pork and beef

In the Vietnamese kitchen, tasty, affordable pork reigns supreme. Many banh mi employ pork, from cold cuts (pages 40 to 53) to the morsels in this chapter. Beef, conversely, is considered a special-occasion treat, to be savored in small, flavorful portions.

grilled lemongrass pork

Makes enough for 6 sandwiches ▪ Takes about 1 hour, plus 1 to 24 hours for marinating

Viet cooks love to grill thinly sliced pork; it's no wonder *banh mi thit nuong* is one of the ubiquitous options at Viet delis. The flavor is often more sweet than savory and dryish in texture. When I make the sandwiches at home, I marinate rich-tasting pork shoulder with elemental southern Viet flavors—lemongrass, garlic, shallot, and fish sauce, then cook it on skewers. It's an easy breezy path toward banh mi heaven.

1½ pounds (675 g) boneless pork shoulder

3 large cloves garlic, chopped

¼ cup (1.1 oz / 35 g) coarsely chopped shallot

1 fat stalk lemongrass, trimmed and coarsely chopped (⅓ cup / 35 g; see page 37)

¼ plus ⅛ teaspoon black pepper

2 tablespoons granulated sugar, or 2½ tablespoons firmly packed light brown sugar

2 teaspoons dark soy sauce, or 1½ teaspoons regular soy sauce plus ½ teaspoon molasses

2 tablespoons fish sauce

1 tablespoon canola oil, plus more for grilling

Cut the pork across the grain into strips, each about 4 to 5 inches (10 to 12.5 cm) long, ¼ inch (6 mm) thick, and 1 inch (2.5 cm) wide (see page 101). Set aside in a bowl.

Put the remaining ingredients in a mini or full-size food processor. Whirl into a semicoarse puree. Pour over the pork, then use your hands to massage and coat the meat well. Thread onto skewers, covering most of each skewer. (With 10-inch / 25-cm bamboo skewers, you'll fill 4 or 5 of them. If you plan to cook on the stove top, cut skewers in half to fit the grill pan, or employ short skewers.) Give each skewer a gentle squeeze so the pork hugs the

skewer and retains its succulence during cooking. Set on a plate, cover, and marinate at room temperature for 1 hour. For best flavor, refrigerate the skewers overnight or up to 24 hours; let sit out at room temperature for 45 minutes to remove some of the chill before grilling.

To cook, prepare a medium-hot charcoal fire, preheat a gas grill to medium-high, or use a stove-top grill pan heated over medium-high heat with a little oil brushed on. Right before grilling, brush oil on the skewers. Cook for about 12 minutes, turning frequently and basting with oil, until the pork is slightly charred and done. Nick a piece to check. Briefly cool before sliding the pork off the skewers. Keep as nuggets or thinly slice to better distribute in sandwiches.

NOTES

This meat goes well with any of the mayonnaises and pickles. Experiment with your **grilled pork banh mi**.

To make grilled lemongrass chicken, use boneless, skinless chicken thighs. Follow the prep and cooking instructions for chicken sate (page 60) but use this marinade.

meatballs in tomato sauce

Makes about 30 meatballs, enough for 6 sandwiches · **Takes about 1¼ hours**

This tasty old school sandwich is a conundrum of sorts. It features delicate Viet meatballs called *xiu mai*, which are inspired by the filling for *shu mai* dumplings, the wildly popular Cantonese dim sum. The fragrant pork mixture is steamed as spheres, then put into a light tomato sauce bath. (Poaching the meatballs in the tomato sauce is my less fussy approach.) To distribute the meat in the bread and construct a sandwich that holds together, banh mi makers mash the meatballs when stuffing them into baguette. Yes, a smashed meatball sandwich based on a dumpling is a crazy-delicious banh mi.

Meatball

1¼ pounds (565 g) ground pork, about 85 percent lean

⅓ cup (2 oz / 60 g) finely chopped yellow onion

½ cup (2.25 oz / 70 g) finely chopped water chestnuts

2 tablespoons finely chopped cilantro sprigs or green onion (green part only)

¼ plus ⅛ teaspoon white pepper

About ½ teaspoon salt

1½ teaspoons sugar

1 tablespoon cornstarch

2 teaspoons toasted sesame oil

1½ tablespoons regular soy sauce

1½ tablespoons Shaoxing rice wine or dry sherry (see page 67)

1 large egg

A 14.5-ounce (410 g) can peeled whole tomatoes in juice (1¾ cups / 420 ml)

1 tablespoon sugar

1 tablespoon ketchup

1 cup (240 ml) water, plus more as needed

2 tablespoons canola oil

½ cup (2 oz / 60 g) chopped shallot

3 large cloves garlic, finely chopped

For the meatballs, in a bowl, combine the pork, onion, water chestnuts, and cilantro, stirring and mashing with a fork. In a smaller bowl, beat together the pepper, salt, sugar, cornstarch, sesame oil, soy sauce, rice wine, and egg. Pour over the meat mixture. Use the fork, a spatula, or your hand to vigorously mix into a sticky, compact mixture. Cover and set aside.

Put the canned tomatoes in a bowl and use your hands to break and mash them up; discard any skin or hard stem ends. Add the 1 tablespoon sugar, ketchup, and water. Set aside.

To cook the sauce and fit all the meatballs in one layer, select a big, wide pan, like a 5-quart (5 l) Dutch oven or deep skillet. Heat it over medium-high heat and add the oil. Add the shallot and cook, stirring frequently, for 2 to 3 minutes, until turning golden. Add the garlic and cook for about 1 minute, until fragrant and no longer raw smelling. Add the tomato mixture.

continued

Bring to a vigorous simmer. With wet hands, form meatballs the size of ping-pong balls (about 1½ tablespoons each), gently dropping them into the bubbling sauce as you work. You'll have about 30 meatballs total; toward the end, gently shake the pan or nudge semicooked meatballs to make room for new ones. When done, all of the meatballs should barely be covered in liquid; add water if needed.

Vigorously simmer for 10 to 20 minutes to cook through and reduce the sauce. When done, the meatballs should be about two-thirds covered by sauce; if you coat the back of a spoon and run your finger through the sauce, a line should hold. Taste and add extra salt, if needed. Cool for about 15 minutes to further concentrate the flavors. Skim the orange oil that gathers at the top or leave it for richness. The warm meatballs are ready for banh mi.

NOTES

Line the bottom of the bread with some sauce and smear mayo on the top portion; drizzle on a little Maggi, if you want. Add the meatballs, breaking and mashing them with your fingers or a spoon to distribute well; or mash the meatballs in the sauce before adding them to the bread. Add any of the pickles, cucumber, cilantro, and chile. Eat your **Vietnamese meatball sandwich** fast or it will get soggy.

To make ahead, cool completely and refrigerate for up to 3 days; warm the meatballs in a saucepan or microwave oven.

chinese barbecued pork

Makes enough for 6 sandwiches · **Takes about 45 minutes, plus 1 to 24 hours for marinating**

Banh mi filled with Chinese barbecued pork (*char siu* in Cantonese, *thit xa xiu* or *xa xiu* in Vietnamese) is a classic. Grill the pork for a more traditional approach or oven roast it for ease. Pork shoulder yields fabulous flavor, but pork tenderloin is simple to butcher.

1½ pounds (675 g) pork tenderloin or boneless pork shoulder

2 cloves garlic, minced and mashed with a knife or put through a garlic press

½ teaspoon Chinese five-spice powder

½ to 1 teaspoon sugar

2 teaspoons toasted sesame oil

1½ tablespoons regular soy sauce

2 tablespoons ketchup

2 tablespoons honey, amber colored and strong flavored preferred

3 tablespoons hoisin sauce

Canola oil, for grilling

Cut the pork into 3 chunky strips. With the tenderloin, cut it crosswise to divide it into even pieces. The pork shoulder will likely yield odd shapes, but aim for strips about 2 inches (5 cm) thick and 6 inches (15 cm) long. Set aside.

In a large bowl, stir together the garlic, five-spice powder, sugar, sesame oil, soy sauce, ketchup, honey, and hoisin. Reserve 2 to 3 tablespoons in a small bowl.

Add the pork to the marinade and turn to coat well. Cover and leave at room temperature for about 1 hour, turning the meat 2 or 3 times. For deeper flavor, transfer to a zip-top plastic bag and refrigerate overnight or up to 24 hours; let sit out at room temperature for 45 minutes to remove some of the chill before cooking.

To grill the pork, prepare a medium charcoal fire or preheat a gas grill to medium. Lightly oil the grates, if needed, then cook for 16 to 20 minutes, turning frequently. During the

last 5 minutes, baste with the reserved marinade; cool on a rack. Alternatively, put the pork on a rack placed in a foil-lined baking sheet, then roast in the top third of an oven preheated to 475°F (245°C / gas mark 9) for 30 to 35 minutes; every 10 minutes, baste with the reserved marinade and turn the meat.

Regardless of cooking method, the pork is done when it looks glazed, is slightly charred, and has an internal temperature of about 145°F (63°C). Let rest for 10 minutes before slicing for sandwiches.

NOTES

Pair the pork with any of the mayos and pickles for **Chinese barbecued pork banh mi**. For a novel take, tuck the sliced pork into banh mi buns (page 117), with a dab of any marinade leftover from cooking or the spicy hoisin sauce (page 31).

The pork is best the day it's cooked, but it can be refrigerated for up to 3 days. Slice and warm in a skillet or microwave. Or keep whole and reheat in a regular oven or toaster oven preheated to 450°F (230°C / gas mark 8) for 10 minutes, turning midway; mix a half batch of the marinade and brush it on during baking to refresh.

For a chicken version, use large boneless, skinless thighs. Butterfly them (see page 58), marinate, and grill over medium heat for 10 to 12 minutes or cook in a grill pan over medium-high heat for 6 to 10 minutes.

caramel sauce pulled pork

Makes enough for 6 sandwiches · **Takes about 2¹/₂ hours**

One of the secret ingredients in Viet cooking is caramel sauce, a bittersweet and reddish-brown staple simply made by nearly burning sugar. Combine caramel sauce with fish sauce in a long-simmered dish and the result is intensely savory-sweet, very umami. In this recipe, grilling and then cooking the pork with caramel sauce creates a wonderful web of flavors. It's a technique handed down from my grandmother. I take it a further step by breaking up the cooked meat and stuffing it into baguette.

2 pounds (900 g) boneless pork shoulder

1¼ cups (5 oz / 150 g) coarsely chopped yellow onion

¾ teaspoon black pepper

1 tablespoon plus ⅓ cup (2.3 oz / 70 g) sugar

3½ tablespoons fish sauce

2 or 3 drops distilled white vinegar or lemon or lime juice (optional, for preventing crystallization)

Cut the pork into chunky pieces, each about half the size of your hand in length and width, and 1½ inches (3.75 cm) thick. Put into a bowl. In a mini or full-size food processor, puree the onion with the pepper, 1 tablespoon of sugar, and 1½ tablespoons of the fish sauce. Pour over the pork and turn to coat well. Cover and marinate for 30 minutes at room temperature.

Meanwhile, make the caramel sauce. Select a 3- to 4-quart (3 to 4 l) saucepan with a light-colored interior (to easily monitor the caramelization). Put 2 tablespoons of water in the pan along with the remaining ⅓ cup (70 g) sugar and the vinegar, if using. Heat over medium heat, stirring with a metal spoon or rubber spatula, until nearly dissolved, about 1 minute. Stop stirring and let the sugar cook.

When the sugar is champagne yellow, after about 4 minutes, pay attention. Swirl the pan to control the caramelization process. Faint smoke should rise in about 1 minute. Keep swirling for another minute or so to coax out a dark tea color.

Turn off the heat and let the sugar continue caramelizing over the burner's residual heat for about 3 minutes, until it's the hue of pinot noir; this caramel is darker than that for the shrimp on page 73. Add 1 cup (240 ml) of water; the sugar will seize up. Set aside.

Prepare a hot charcoal fire or preheat a gas grill to high. Remove the pork from the marinade, reserving the marinade, and sear each piece on all sides, turning as needed, for about 8 minutes total. A few charred edges and grill marks are good. (Or put the meat on a foil-lined baking sheet and broil as close to the heat as possible for 4 to 5 minutes per side, until tinged with brown and a bit charred.)

Heat the pan with the caramel sauce over high heat, stirring to dissolve the sugar. Add the seared pork, any cooking juices, the reserved marinade, and the remaining 2 tablespoons fish sauce. As needed, add water to almost cover. Bring to a boil, lower the heat to a simmer, cover, and cook for 45 minutes.

Uncover and adjust the heat to vigorously simmer. Cook for 25 minutes, or until the meat is tender when pierced with the tip of a knife. A generous amount of sauce should remain.

Remove from the heat and cool for 15 minutes. Transfer the meat to a skillet, reserving the cooking liquid to flavor the bread and pork. Use a potato masher and maybe your fingers to break the meat into pieces; discard lingering fat or gristle.

If using the pork right away, add about ⅓ cup (90 ml) of the cooking liquid to the skillet. Cook over medium heat, stirring occasionally, until the liquid has been absorbed.

This intensifies the pork's flavor, readying it for sandwiches. When preparing in advance, refrigerate the pork and cooking liquid in separate containers for up to 3 days. Reheat and flavor the meat before using.

NOTE

To build your **Vietnamese pulled pork banh mi**, moisten the bottom portion of bread with the cooking liquid (warm first, as needed). Spread any of the mayos on the top portion of bread and drizzle on Maggi or more cooking liquid. Add the pork and all the fixings. The pork is perfect for stuffing into steamed buns (page 117) too.

crispy roast pork

Makes enough for 6 sandwiches ▪ **Takes about 2 hours, plus 24 to 36 hours of refrigeration**

Decadent and delicious, baguette filled with rich roast pork and its crackly skin is the Viet equivalent of an Italian porchetta sandwich. Chinese barbecue shops sell the pork (*thit heo quay*), but make your own to select the cut, control the flavor, and ensure lots of crispy skin.

You need pork with fat and skin intact—a piece that lies relatively flat to evenly expose the skin to the oven heat. Boneless cuts like lean boneless belly (lean side pork), pork leg (fresh ham), or picnic shoulder are ideal. Belly and leg are sold at Chinese and Vietnamese markets; some supermarkets sell fresh hams and picnic shoulder roasts.

Choose a slab of pork belly with a healthy layer of fat right below the skin and an even distribution of fat and lean. For the leg or shoulder cuts, select a piece about 4 inches (10 cm) wide; you usually have to trim a portion of flesh uncovered by skin, so start with a fairly large piece. Prep the pork 24 to 36 hours in advance to give the skin time to sufficiently dry.

3 large cloves garlic, minced and mashed or put through a press

¼ plus ⅛ teaspoon white pepper

Salt, fine sea salt preferred

¾ teaspoon Chinese five-spice powder

1 tablespoon firmly packed light or dark brown sugar

1 teaspoon regular soy sauce

About 2¼ pounds (1 kg) skin-on, boneless lean pork belly, or 4 pounds (1.8 kg) skin-on boneless pork leg or picnic shoulder

In a small bowl, stir together the garlic, pepper, ¾ teaspoon of salt, five-spice powder, sugar, and soy sauce. Taste and adjust the flavor for a strong salty-sweet-pungent finish. Set aside.

If using the belly, cut it into 2 square pieces. If using the leg or shoulder, trim the ends of any flesh not covered by fat and skin. To force the pork to sit flat, trim the flesh on the bottom to even out; smack the skin side to make sure the whole piece sits well. Then cut the pork crosswise into 2 shorter chunky strips. (Save trimmings for lemongrass pork on page 84.)

Regardless of the cut, use a sharp knife to score the skin crosswise at intervals roughly ½ to ¾ inch (1.25 to 2 cm) apart. Cut through the skin and deep into the fat, but avoid cutting into the meat; rub a generous ½ teaspoon of salt into the skin and between the score lines of each piece. Discard salt that falls off.

With the skin side down, rub the seasoning paste on the flesh and fat. Wipe off any paste from the skin. Place the pork skin side up on a rack set on a baking sheet. Refrigerate, uncovered, for 24 to 36 hours, until the skin has dried out, darkened, and shrunk to reveal the fat between the score marks. The pork is ready when the skin feels leathery, even a bit hard. Roasting before the skin sufficiently dries just means that it won't be as crackly. Once ready, the pork can stay refrigerated for a day longer; if needed, loosely cover to prevent overdrying.

continued

Remove the pork from the refrigerator and transfer the rack and pork to a foil-lined baking sheet. If a piece is lopsided, prop it up with foil to level the top surface. Let the pork sit at room temperature for 30 to 45 minutes to remove the chill.

Position a rack in the middle of the oven and preheat to 325°F (170°C / gas mark 3). Right before roasting, lift and push up any edges of skin that curved down during chilling; a flat layer of skin is best. Roast the pork for about 1¼ hours, or until rich brown and tender; poke a skewer ½ inch (1.25 cm) into the fat to check. The skin may blister a bit toward the end of the roasting time.

Now broil for 4 to 10 minutes to force the skin to bubble and puff, forming a lovely layer of cracklings. Be vigilant at this stage. Leave the pork in the middle of the oven to avoid burning the skin. If your broiler element is under the oven, drain any fat before broiling. Expect pops, hisses, and rivulets of melting fat. If patches of unblistered skin remain, carefully broil the pork about 4 inches (10 cm) away from the heat source for about 30 seconds. A little charring is okay.

Remove the pork from the oven, and let it rest for at least 10 minutes. Enjoy hot, warm, or at room temperature, cutting the pork along the score lines and then crosswise into finger-size pieces, if you like, to easily eat in a sandwich.

NOTES

Roast pork banh mi can be as simple as sliding the pork inside baguette with a light sprinkling of salt and lots of black pepper. For sauce, mix 2 tablespoons of soy sauce with 1 tablespoon of water and drizzle that onto the bread. Mayo is not generally needed, unless you add all the vegetable garnishes and the upper portion of bread needs to be moistened. For fun, lay out the options and let guests compose their own **Viet roast pork sandwich** (*banh mi thit heo quay*).

Refrigerate and reheat uncut pork in a regular or toaster oven preheated to 350°F (180° or 175°C / gas mark 4) until hot, about 15 minutes. If the skin needs recrisping, broil it for 2 to 3 minutes.

viet home-style doner kebab

Makes enough for 6 sandwiches ▪ **Takes 1 hour, plus cooling time or an overnight chill**

How did the doner kebab, a wildly popular Turkish-German sandwich, become a banh mi? By way of Tran Minh Ngoc, a chef who worked in Germany in the late 1990s and opened the first doner kebab grill in 2005 after returning to Hanoi.

Because of local preferences, the Viet version features pork—not beef, veal, or lamb as is often used in Germany. In Vietnam, the meat is cooked on a vertical spit like shawarma; I simply bake a free-form, cumin-scented pork meatloaf. It works like a charm.

2 cloves garlic, coarsely chopped

⅔ cup (3 oz / 90 g) coarsely chopped yellow onion

¼ teaspoon black pepper

¼ teaspoon cayenne

¾ teaspoon salt

2 teaspoons ground cumin

Generous 1 teaspoon cornstarch

1½ tablespoons all-purpose flour, rice flour (brown or white), or almond meal flour

1 large egg

2 tablespoons canola or olive oil

1¼ pounds (565 g) ground pork, about 85 percent lean

1 teaspoon regular soy sauce mixed with ½ teaspoon water

Position a rack in the middle of the oven and preheat to 425°F (220°C / gas mark 7). Line a baking sheet with foil and set aside.

Place the garlic, onion, pepper, cayenne, salt, cumin, cornstarch, flour, egg, and oil in the bowl of a food processor and whirl to create a finely textured, soupy mixture. Scrape down the sides, then add the pork, dropping it in as large chunks. Restart the processor to combine, letting it run for about 5 seconds after the meat begins gathering around the blade. Aim to mix things as if you were making a meatloaf. Visible bits of pork are good! Use a spatula to scrape and mix in seasonings clinging to the processor walls.

Transfer the meat to the prepared baking sheet and shape it into a slab, about 1¼ inches (3 cm) thick, 5 inches (12.5 cm) wide, and 8 inches (20 cm) long. For a lovely brown crust, use your fingers to paint the top and sides with the diluted soy mixture.

Bake for 35 to 40 minutes, until the top is redwood tree brown and small sizzling bubbles appear. The meat will puff and maybe bend upward slightly. Cool completely before thinly slicing, or better yet, cool, wrap, and chill overnight or for as long as 3 days.

Cut the meat cold and warm in a microwave oven or in a skillet over medium heat. Don't fret if the meat slices break, just slide it all into your sandwich.

NOTES

When crafting a **doner kebab banh mi**, line the bottom of the bread with garlic yogurt sauce (page 29) and the top portion of bread with Sriracha aïoli (page 26) and/or Sriracha sauce. From the bottom up, add the meat, citrusy red cabbage pickle (page 34), soft lettuce leaf or shredded iceberg lettuce, tomato slices, cucumber slices or strips, and chopped cilantro. Offer Sriracha on the side.

For richness, embellish with homemade fried shallots or canned French-fried onions.

beef and curry sliders

Makes patties for 12 sliders, for 4 to 6 people ▪ Takes about 30 minutes

When my family first arrived in America, hamburgers were a novelty food that we'd enjoy for a special Sunday brunch. My mother panfried the patties and we'd dress them up with all the fixings to resemble the magazine photos and billboards that whetted our appetites.

Nowadays, I make these mini cross-cultural patties—a heady combination of ground beef, Indian curry powder, Chinese oyster sauce, and Vietnamese fish sauce. They are perfect for banh mi sliders.

1½ pounds (675 g) ground beef, 80 percent lean preferred

2 cloves garlic, minced and mashed with a knife blade or put through a press

⅓ cup (2 oz / 60 g) finely chopped yellow onion

¼ plus ⅛ teaspoon salt

Rounded 1 teaspoon black pepper

1 tablespoon Madras curry powder

2 teaspoons fish sauce

1 tablespoon oyster sauce

About 2 tablespoons canola oil

Put the beef in a bowl and add the garlic and onion. Use a fork to gently mix and loosen the beef. Add the salt, pepper, curry powder, fish sauce, and oyster sauce. Mix with the fork to combine well, taking care not to compress the ingredients.

Shape the meat into 12 patties, about ½ inch (1.25 cm) thick and slightly bigger than your mini buns; they will shrink. Be gentle or the patties will compact too much and not cook up to a nice juiciness. To prevent sticking, brush or rub oil on the patties.

To cook, heat a heavy skillet or stove-top grill pan brushed with a little oil over medium-high heat and cook the patties in batches, about 2 minutes on the first side. The second side needs about 1 minute for medium-rare, 1½ minutes for medium. Let rest and cool for a few minutes before assembling the sliders.

NOTES

See page 10 for how to assemble sliders.

For extra richness, spread Laughing Cow cheese (a part of Vietnam's colonial past) atop the patties after cooking.

Apply the garlic yogurt sauce (page 29) and other garnishes for the doner kebab (page 95) and you have a Vietnamese-American-Turkish-German treat.

star anise and lemongrass sloppy joe

Makes enough for 6 sandwiches · Takes about 1 hour

In 2012, I tasted a "Sloppy Bao" at Baoguette in Manhattan and thought of creating a banh mi filled with spicy ground beef. I eventually created this, a riff on *bo kho*, the classic Viet-Franco stew of beef, star anise, and lemongrass in a tomatoey sauce that's often served with baguette on the side. Here, I turn the stew into a sloppy Joe–like mixture for a sensational banh mi.

1¼ pounds (565 g) ground beef, chuck preferred

2 cloves garlic, chopped

Hefty 1-inch (2.5-cm) knob ginger, peeled and coarsely chopped

1 large red chile, such as Fresno or cayenne, coarsely chopped (keep seeds intact)

1 medium stalk lemongrass, trimmed and coarsely chopped (¼ cup / 30 g; see page 37)

¾ cup (3.5 oz / 115 g) coarsely chopped shallots

A 14.5-ounce (410 g) can peeled whole tomatoes in juice (1¾ cups / 420 ml)

2 tablespoons canola oil

1 bay leaf

2 star anise

¼ teaspoon salt

1 teaspoon Chinese five-spice powder

1½ teaspoons packed light or dark brown sugar

1½ tablespoons fish sauce

1 medium carrot (4 oz / 120 g), peeled and finely chopped or coarsely grated

Coarsely chop the ground beef to loosen. Set aside. In a food processor, mince the garlic, ginger, chile, lemongrass, and shallot. Transfer to a bowl. Reuse the processor to puree the tomatoes and their juice. Set aside.

In a large saucepan, heat the oil over medium-high heat. Add the shallot mixture and cook for about 2 minutes, stirring frequently, until fragrant and no longer raw smelling.

Raise the heat to high, add the beef and mash and stir to break it up. Cook for 1 to 2 minutes, until mostly browned, then add the bay leaf, star anise, salt, five-spice powder, brown sugar, and fish sauce. Cook for 1 to 2 minutes, until the beef is aromatic with the seasonings.

Add the carrot and tomato. Bring to a simmer, cover, and cook for 15 minutes, stirring occasionally. Uncover and adjust the heat to vigorously simmer and reduce the sauce, about 15 minutes. When done, there should be little liquid left and the beef should mostly hold its shape when scooped up by a spoon. Let rest, uncovered, for 15 minutes to meld flavors.

Taste and adjust the flavor as needed with salt or a glug of fish sauce, or splash in water to loosen or lighten. Discard the bay leaf and star anise before making banh mi.

NOTES

Construct a **Vietnamese sloppy Joe** as banh mi or sliders (see page 10). Because the beef mixture is moist, spread regular mayo or Sriracha aïoli (pages 24 and 26) on only the top portion of bread. Drizzle on the Maggi. Spoon on the beef, then add the other ingredients. Instead of cilantro, try chopped fresh Thai or Italian basil or Vietnamese coriander (*rau ram*).

The beef can be refrigerated for up to 2 days. Warm in a pan or microwave oven, then use.

Feel free to substitute ½ teaspoon dried red chile flakes or paprika for the fresh chile. If you bought a large can of tomatoes, use the leftover for the pork meatballs (page 87) and vice versa. You'll be a bit short, so add water to compensate.

STAR ANISE AND LEMONGRASS
SLOPPY JOE

BEEF AND CURRY SLIDERS

KOREAN BEEF
AND KIMCHI

GINGERY TOFU
SLIDERS

korean beef and kimchi

Makes enough for 6 sandwiches ▪ **Takes about 45 minutes, plus 2 hours for marinating**

This recipe comes from Yun Ho Rhee, a terrific home cook and former corporate executive in Seoul. His family lived in Saigon in the 1960s, an experience that seeded his love of Viet food. He's been making this marvelous sandwich for years, marrying the best of Korean and Viet traditions. The beef tends to weep liquid during cooking so I sear it in batches and cook the marinade ingredients down. See Notes (page 100) for meat sourcing.

1 pound (450 g) very thinly sliced beef sirloin or rump

½ large yellow onion, thinly sliced (4 oz / 120 g)

2 green onions, white and green parts, thinly cut on the diagonal

Rounded 2 teaspoons raw white or brown sesame seeds

¾ teaspoon black pepper

Scant 2 tablespoons sugar

3 large cloves garlic, coarsely chopped

1 tablespoon toasted sesame oil

1½ tablespoons sake or dry sherry

3 tablespoons regular soy sauce

About 2 tablespoons canola oil

1½ cups (12 oz / 350 g) drained napa cabbage kimchi, cut into bite-size pieces

If the beef is thicker than ⅛ inch (3 mm), pound each slice between pieces of waxed paper or plastic wrap with a meat tenderizer or saucepan. Cut the beef to roughly the size of your hand. Put in a bowl and add the onion and green onion. Set aside.

In a small saucepan or skillet over medium heat, toast the sesame seeds for 2 to 3 minutes, shaking or stirring frequently, until lightly colored; unhulled seeds may pop. Cool off of the heat for several minutes before transferring to a mini food processor. Add the pepper and sugar, then grind to a fragrant, sandy mixture. Add the garlic, sesame oil, wine, and soy sauce. Whirl into a relatively smooth, liquid marinade.

Pour the marinade over the beef. Use your hand to massage all the ingredients until little visible liquid remains. Cover and refrigerate for 2 hours, or as long as 24 hours. Before cooking, let sit at room temperature for 30 minutes to remove the chill.

Heat a large cast-iron or heavy nonstick skillet over high or medium-high heat. Add 1 teaspoon of oil and cook the beef in batches, leaving the onion in the bowl. Spread each slice out flat and flip after about 30 seconds, when the beef has browned on the underside. Cook the second side until the beef starts releasing liquid and flutters, about 20 seconds. Transfer to a plate, wiping the skillet bottom with the beef to pick up extra flavor or color. Push any super brown bits left in the skillet to the side or add them to the plate. Add oil and repeat with the remaining beef, adjusting the heat as needed.

After searing the beef, lower the heat slightly and add 1 tablespoon of oil to the skillet. Add all the onion and remaining marinade. Cook, stirring, until the onions no longer smell raw, about 2 minutes. Add the cooking juices from the plate of beef. Cook until the onions have absorbed most of the liquid and are a chestnut brown. Off the heat, combine the onion with the beef. Cut the beef into bite-size pieces and employ with the kimchi to make banh mi.

continued

NOTES

For a **Korean beef and kimchi banh mi**, line the bread with the regular mayo or Sriracha aïoli (pages 24 and 26); omit Maggi. Add the beef, about $1/4$ cup (2 oz / 60 g) of kimchi, cucumber, and cilantro. If you don't have kimchi, substitute one of the pickles.

To create a **Korean cheesesteak banh mi**, reheat the cut-up beef in a skillet or on a griddle, and after it is hot, arrange it as a flat pile, then put sliced mozzarella (or other meltable cheese) on top. Warm kimchi on another part of the pan. Line a roll with mayo, then fill it with the cheesy beef and kimchi. Add chopped cilantro and eat warm.

Refrigerate leftovers for up to 3 days and reheat in a skillet over high heat.

Korean markets sell a wealth of presliced beef. At mainstream markets, shop for thinly sliced beef for stir-frying or carne asada. You can also use a favorite steak cut, freezing it for about 30 minutes before very thinly cutting it across the grain (see opposite).

maggi steaks

Makes enough for 4 or 5 sandwiches · **Takes about 45 minutes**

These are the steaks (*bit-tet*) of my childhood, marinated with lots of garlic, black pepper, and Maggi Seasoning sauce. Like countless other Viet cooks, I panfry it for a nice outside crust of flavor, then thinly slice the beef and serve it with rice for dinner. My husband typically benefits from the leftovers, which I turn into a steak banh mi for him to take to work. One day I asked myself, what about *my* steak banh mi lunch? Life is too short to always wait for leftovers.

2 top sirloin, tri-tip (bottom sirloin), or New York strip (top loin) steaks, each about 10 ounces (300 g) and 1 inch (2.5 cm) thick

2 large cloves garlic, minced and mashed or put through a press

¼ plus ⅛ teaspoon black pepper

1½ tablespoons Maggi Seasoning sauce, mock Maggi sauce (page 30), or regular soy sauce

1½ tablespoons canola oil

Salt

Trim the steaks of any gristle. Set aside. On a plate large enough to accommodate the steaks, combine the garlic, pepper, Maggi, and oil. Taste and add salt, if needed. Coat the steaks well in the marinade. Set aside for 30 minutes, turning the steaks over midway.

Heat a medium heavy-bottomed or cast-iron skillet over medium heat until a drop of water flicked on it immediately dances and then evaporates. Add the steaks and let them cook, undisturbed, for 6 minutes. They should be well browned on the underside. Use tongs to turn them over. Cook the second side, undisturbed, for another 4 minutes for rare, 5 minutes for medium-rare, and 6 minutes for medium. Check doneness by nicking a steak with the tip of a paring knife.

Transfer the steaks to a plate and let rest, uncovered, for 5 minutes. Thinly slice across the grain for sandwiches. Tumble the meat in its juices for extra flavor.

NOTE

Build your **Maggi steak banh mi** like any other, but go light on the Maggi because there's some in the beef already. Drizzle the cooking juices onto the bread, if you like. The beef goes with any of the pickles and mayos, though the Maggi and cilantro one may overwhelm. Also, try the garlic yogurt sauce (page 29).

going against the grain

Cutting meat against the grain can make it easier to chew. Figure out which way the muscle fibers run and start cutting across their path. If the grain changes direction, turn the meat. Wield your knife at a 45-degree angle for broad, luxurious pieces.

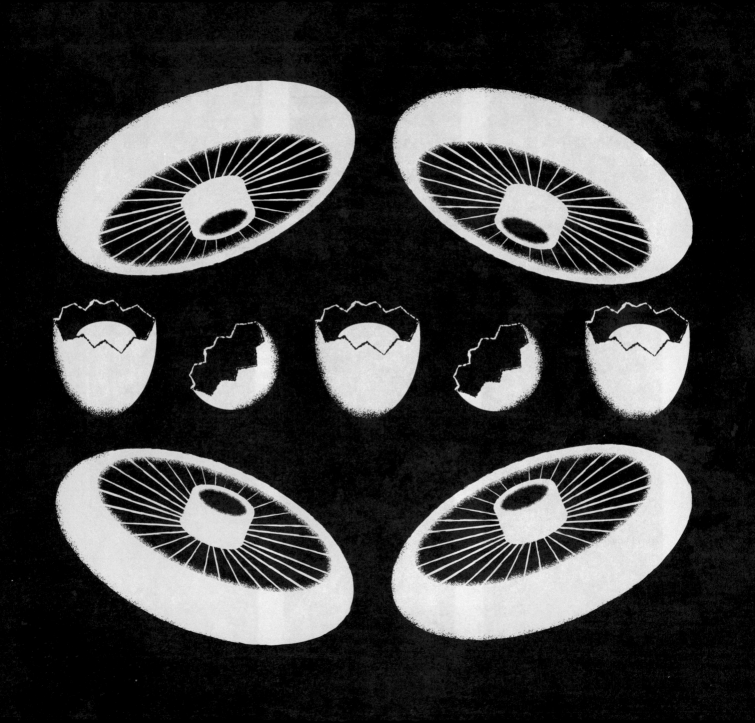

vegetarian

Many Vietnamese sandwiches are meat-centric affairs, but there are wonderful meatless ones to try. Instead of the traditional vegetarian options of sunny-side-up eggs, lemongrass tofu, and vegetarian pork skin (*bi chay*)—you can figure out the first and I've published the other two in *Asian Tofu*—try these six recipes for something delectable and different.

Meatless Asian dishes sometimes employ fish sauce for flavor. If you enjoy a pure vegetarian diet, use the suggested substitute.

peppery portobello

Makes enough for 4 sandwiches ▪ **Takes about 25 minutes**

Meaty portobello mushrooms can be featured alone or combined with a protein for extra satisfying banh mi. I like to cook the mushrooms in a cast-iron grill pan—when marinade drips onto the hot pan it caramelizes and the mushroom caps pick up that deliciousness. This super easy, versatile banh mi filling can be made days ahead.

4 portobello mushrooms, each 4 to 5 inches (10 to 12.5 cm) wide

¼ teaspoon sugar

Rounded ¼ teaspoon salt

1 to 1¼ teaspoons black pepper

1 tablespoon fresh lime juice

1 tablespoon regular soy sauce

3 tablespoons canola oil

Rub any dirt bits from the mushrooms, then gently break off the stems. The dark gills may stain your sandwich; scrape them off with a teaspoon if you like. Set aside.

In a bowl, combine the sugar, salt, pepper, lime juice, and soy sauce. Taste and adjust as needed for a tangy, peppery, salty finish. Add the oil and set the seasonings near the stove.

Heat a grill pan over medium-high or high heat. Brush seasonings on the curved side of each mushroom cap, then place it gill side up in the grill pan and brush seasonings on the gill side. Cook for 5 minutes, turn over, then cook for another 5 minutes, basting with the remaining seasonings. Steam will shoot from under the caps as they cook gill sides down.

Flip and cook for 3 to 5 minutes longer, basting and flipping the caps frequently and pressing on the caps with a spatula to flatten and force greater contact with the hot pan. The caps should end up half their original thickness and chewy-soft. Cool gill side down and use slightly warm or at room temperature for sandwiches. Or refrigerate for up to 3 days, slicing and refreshing the mushrooms in the microwave oven.

NOTES

Keep the mushroom caps whole or cut like a steak into thin pieces; quarter them for sliders. Assemble your **peppery portobello banh mi** as you would a typical Viet sandwich. Or, whip up a pickled shallot and arugula or watercress salad (page 36) and sub it for the regular vegetables.

For protein, spread on some edamame pâté (page 48), or add baked Maggi tofu, coconut curry tofu, or egg and tofu pancakes (pages 53, 108, and 107, respectively). A smearing of Laughing Cow cheese on the bottom layer is good too.

If portobellos are not available, use extra-large white mushrooms or cremini (baby portobello) and cut down on the cooking time.

gingery tofu sliders

Makes 10 to 12 sliders, to serve 3 or 4 · Takes about 1 hour

There's plenty of flavor here to satisfy without weighing you down. Look for tofu made from organic and/or non-GMO soybeans, and check the best-by date for the freshest package. Opt for the long marination to allow flavors to penetrate; make mayo or a pickle while the tofu sits. (Pictured on page 98.)

14 to 16 ounces (400 to 450 g) firm or super-firm tofu

Pinch of black pepper

2 teaspoons honey

1 to 1½ teaspoons fresh ginger juice (see Notes)

2 to 2½ tablespoons regular soy sauce

1 tablespoon toasted sesame oil

1 tablespoon canola oil, plus more as needed

Cut the tofu lengthwise into thick slabs, each ½ to ¾ inch (1.25 to 2 cm) thick. Then cut each slab crosswise to form squarish pieces, about the size of your slider buns or rolls. You should have 10 or 12 pieces. Put the tofu on a non-terry dishtowel or double layer of paper towels set atop a plate to partially drain while you make the marinade.

Select a baking pan or dish that can fit all the tofu pieces in one layer; 9 by 13-inch (22.5 by 32.5-cm) works. In that dish, stir together the pepper, honey, ginger juice, and soy sauce. Taste and adjust the flavors, as needed. Add the sesame oil and 1 tablespoon canola oil, stirring to combine. Add the tofu, turning each piece to coat well. Marinate for 30 to 45 minutes or as long as 2 hours, turning every 15 minutes or so.

To cook the tofu, use a heavy nonstick skillet or a stovetop grill pan. Brush oil on the grill pan (no oil is needed for the skillet), then heat the pan over medium-high or high heat until hot—when water flicked into the pan evaporates in seconds. Sear the tofu for about 2 minutes per side in a skillet, or 3 minutes on a grill pan, turning with one or two thin spatulas, until the tofu has some dark chestnut browning. Cool on a rack for a few minutes before making the sliders.

NOTES

See page 10 for guidance on assembling **tofu banh mi sliders**. These tofu pieces are soft on the inside so don't overtoast the bread, or the sliders won't hold together well. Mini pita pockets would work here.

To extract ginger juice, grate unpeeled fresh ginger with a Microplane or Japanese grater, then press the solids through a fine-mesh strainer to obtain the cloudy yellow liquid. A chubby 1-inch (2.5-cm) knob of ginger yields about a teaspoon of juice.

egg and tofu pancakes

Makes 8 pancakes, enough for 4 sandwiches · Takes about 20 minutes

These egg pancakes are a little crispy at the edges (from added cornstarch) and wonderfully savory; their shape and size make them perfect for banh mi. They are fast to prepare and reheat well, so you can make some *trung chien dau hu* for now or later.

⅛ teaspoon salt

⅛ teaspoon black pepper

2 teaspoons cornstarch

2 teaspoons regular soy sauce

4 large eggs

3 green onions, white and green parts, chopped

8 ounces (225 g) firm tofu

Canola oil, for frying

In a bowl, combine the salt, pepper, cornstarch, and soy sauce, stirring to dissolve the cornstarch. Add the eggs and beat to combine well. Add the green onions and set aside.

Break up the tofu into 3 or 4 chunks. Working in batches, put the tofu in a non-terry dishtowel or piece of muslin, then gather it up. Standing over a sink, firmly squeeze and massage the tofu; unwrap. Stir gently into the egg mixture to combine. You should have a scant 2 cups (480 ml).

Pour enough oil into a medium or large nonstick skillet to thinly coat the bottom. Heat over medium-high heat until a drop of egg immediately sizzles and blooms upon contact with the oil. To make each pancake, scoop up a scant ¼ cup (60 ml) of the egg mixture and pour into the skillet; don't worry about a perfect shape. Fry 3 or 4 pancakes at a time to avoid overcrowding.

When the edges of a pancake are set and lightly browned, about 2 minutes, use a spatula to turn it. Fry for another 1 to 2 minutes, until browned on the second side. If you like, refry the first side for about 30 seconds to reinforce the crisp edges. Cool on a rack. Repeat to fry more, adding extra oil as needed to maintain a gentle sizzle around the rim of each pancake. These are good warm or at room temperature in banh mi.

NOTES

Cut the pancakes to fit inside the bread and assemble an **egg and tofu pancake banh mi** like a typical Viet sandwich.

These pancakes can be refrigerated for several days and reheated in a toaster oven preheated to 400°F (200°C) for about 5 minutes, flipping midway.

coconut curry tofu

Makes 6 pieces, for 3 or 4 sandwiches · Takes about 30 minutes, plus 15 minutes to cool

Tofu is a mainstay in Vietnamese kitchens, not just for vegetarians but for everyone. I often panfry or deep-fry tofu to create a toothsome texture, then simmer or stir-fry it with other ingredients that imbue the tofu with flavor. When making banh mi, I simplify things and simmer the tofu with seasonings and a bit of oil. After the seasonings cook down, they leave the tofu to panfry to a delicate crustiness. Coconut and curry powder, staples used for Indian-inflected Viet dishes, are distilled in these spicy-sweet morsels. This recipe uses fish sauce, but you can substitute soy sauce for a vegetarian version.

14 to 16 ounces (400 to 450 g) firm or super-firm tofu

1 teaspoon packed light or dark brown sugar

1 teaspoon curry powder

2 teaspoons fish sauce or regular soy sauce

3 tablespoons coconut cream

Salt

1 tablespoon virgin coconut or canola oil

Cut the tofu crosswise into rectangular slabs, each about ¾ inch (2 cm) thick. Put the tofu on a non-terry dishtowel or double layer of paper towels set atop a plate to partially drain for 5 minutes.

Meanwhile, in a medium nonstick skillet, stir together the sugar, curry powder, fish sauce, and coconut cream. Taste and adjust the flavor to be savory and spicy; if it needs saltiness, add fish sauce or salt rather than more soy sauce, which may darken the tofu too much. Add the tofu, turning it to coat both sides. Add the coconut oil, which will melt as the pan heats, or drizzle in the oil.

Heat the skillet over medium-high heat. After things start vigorously bubbling, cook for 15 to 20 minutes, using two spatulas to turn the tofu every 3 minutes or so to evenly cook and brown; it will spit gently midway through as the liquid evaporates. Turn the tofu more frequently toward the end to sear the pieces further; it's done when the edges are dark brown (the center remains soft). Some spicy solids will cling to the tofu; scrape up any lingering bits to add to your sandwich.

Cool the tofu on a rack for about 15 minutes before using. Enjoy warm or at room temperature. Hold your knife at a 45-degree angle to cut beautiful, broad slices for sandwiches.

NOTES

If you want to echo soybeans and curry, add a smearing of edamame pâté (page 48) to your **coconut curry tofu banh mi**. All the mayonnaises and pickles pair well with the tofu. Use eggless mayonnaise (page 28) or avocado to build a vegan sandwich.

Buy coconut cream or scoop it from the thick, creamy plug of an unshaken can of coconut milk.

thai fried omelet

Makes enough for 1 sandwich · Takes 5 minutes

With two eggs on hand, you can make a fried egg banh mi (*banh mi trung*)—breakfast for many people and my own favorite anytime food. The default is to make sunny-side up eggs or a French-style omelet, but I like to fry the eggs Thai style, in hot oil, for a fluffy, golden brown omelet with a bit of crispness. It's brilliant, simple cooking.

2 pinches of black or white pepper

1 teaspoon cornstarch

1 teaspoon fish sauce or soy sauce

1 teaspoon water

2 large eggs, at room temperature

3 to 4 tablespoons canola oil

In a bowl, stir or whisk together the pepper, cornstarch, fish sauce, and water. Add the eggs and beat or whisk well to combine. Set aside.

Heat a wok or a small nonstick skillet over medium heat. Add oil to thickly film the bottom (thick as a bean sprout). Heat until the oil is very hot, nearly smoking; a drop of egg dabbed into the oil should immediately sizzle and bloom.

Pour in the egg (from as high as 12 inches / 30 cm if you love drama). It should spread and puff like a self-inflating raft. Use a spatula to pull and push the edges toward the middle, allowing excess egg to flow out into the oil to expand the size of the omelet. Expect a crazy shape and uneven texture.

When the omelet has nearly set (it's still wet but not jiggly), raise the heat to medium-high or high. Fry for about 1 minute, until the edges are golden and the bottom browns a bit. Use one or two spatulas to flip the omelet over. Cook for 30 to 60 seconds longer, or until the bottom picks up some browning. If you like, briefly refry the first side.

Drain and cool the omelet on a rack. Blot excess oil with paper towels, if you like, then fold it over before sliding into bread for banh mi.

NOTES

Let this omelet fly solo in a **Thai fried omelet banh mi** with all the fixings, or use it with another filling, such as the grilled portobello (page 105) or the sardine and tomato sauce (page 76). Make 3 or 4 omelets for a round of banh mi lettuce wraps (page 120), cutting the omelet into bite-size pieces and drizzling on some spicy hoisin sauce (page 31).

Revive a cold omelet in a toaster oven preheated to 375°F (190°C) for 5 to 6 minutes, flipping midway.

lemongrass sriracha tempeh

Makes about 18 ounces (510 g), enough for 6 sandwiches · **Takes about 1 hour, plus 2 to 24 hours to marinate**

My friend Randy Clemens is obsessed with Sriracha, having written two popular cookbooks celebrating the Thai chile sauce. He contributed this tasty recipe, which calls for marinating and twice baking tempeh slices to render them tender and super flavorful. Shop for tempeh at natural foods markets where it's often displayed near tofu, its kin.

2 (8 oz / 225 g) packages tempeh, all soybean or with grains

3 cloves garlic, coarsely chopped

Hefty 1-inch (2.5 cm) chunk fresh ginger, peeled and coarsely chopped

4 green onions, white part only, coarsely chopped

1 medium stalk lemongrass, trimmed and coarsely chopped (¼ cup / 30 g; see page 37)

About 2 tablespoons fresh lime juice

2 tablespoons canola oil, plus more as needed

About ¼ cup (60 ml) Sriracha sauce

¼ cup (60 ml) Maggi Seasoning sauce or mock Maggi sauce (page 30)

1½ cups (360 ml) water

Virgin coconut or canola oil (optional)

Cut the tempeh crosswise into slices, each a scant ½ inch (1.25 cm) thick. Arrange flat in a baking dish, such as a 3-quart (3 l) glass pan suitable for lasagna. Make a partial second layer, as needed. Set aside.

For the marinade, use a food processor to mince the garlic, ginger, green onion, and lemongrass. Add the lime juice, 2 tablespoons of oil, Sriracha, Maggi, and water. Pulse to blend. Taste, and if you like high heat and acidity, add an extra tablespoon of Sriracha and lime juice. Pour over the tempeh. Cover and let sit for 2 hours. Or refrigerate overnight, returning to room temperature before moving on.

Position a rack in the middle of the oven and preheat to 375°F (190°C / gas mark 5). Bake the tempeh, uncovered, for 30 minutes. Meanwhile, line a large baking sheet with parchment paper.

Remove the tempeh from the oven but keep the oven on. Cool for a few minutes, then use a spatula to transfer the tempeh to the prepared baking sheet, arranging the slices flat; if a side is coated with seasoning solids, let it face up. Pour the marinade into a medium saucepan and boil for 5 to 8 minutes, until reduced by nearly half and resembling barbecue sauce. Set aside.

Meanwhile, bake the tempeh for 10 minutes. Flip, then brush on the reduced marinade, saving the leftover. Bake for 10 minutes longer, or until the slices look dry and are slightly burnt orange-red. Cool for 10 minutes before using, or cool completely and refrigerate in an airtight container for up to 3 days; freeze it for up to a month.

Enjoy slightly warm to savor the tempeh's natural umami. Or sear the tempeh over medium-high heat in a nonstick skillet with a light film of coconut or canola oil. You only need about 30 seconds per side to pick up a slight crispness and a bit of browning.

NOTES

When building a **lemongrass Sriracha tempeh banh mi**, lay down the mayo, then smear leftover marinade on the bottom portion of bread; season the top portion of bread with Maggi. Include the usual elements but skip fresh chile if the Sriracha heat is enough.

Instead of tempeh, substitute 1 to 1¼ pounds (450 to 565 g) of super-firm tofu. Cut it crosswise into ½-inch (1.25-cm) slabs and follow the directions in the baked Maggi tofu recipe (page 53) to press out moisture. Because of the higher density of the tofu and the size of the pieces, marinate overnight before baking as directed above. Slice for banh mi.

when to eat banh mi?

Many people think of banh mi as midday fare, but in Vietnam banh mi vendors—ranging from those selling via street carts and tiny neighborhood joints to those with baskets slung on shoulder poles—do a brisk morning business. The sandwiches make for a satisfying breakfast, especially paired with Viet coffee and sweetened condensed milk. Such vendors may keep hours from 7 to 10 am, or until they run out of bread.

Others then take over to ensure that customers can have a banh mi lunch or afternoon snack. Nighttime banh mi noshes are a tad harder to find in Vietnam but they are there, with vendors usually situated near a street light or well-lit corner. And just like abroad, there are largish banh mi shops in Vietnam that maintain long hours. Friends in Saigon took me to one that's open 24/7—a testament to people's love of the sandwich.

Now that you know all the possibilities, knock yourself out. There's a banh mi for every moment.

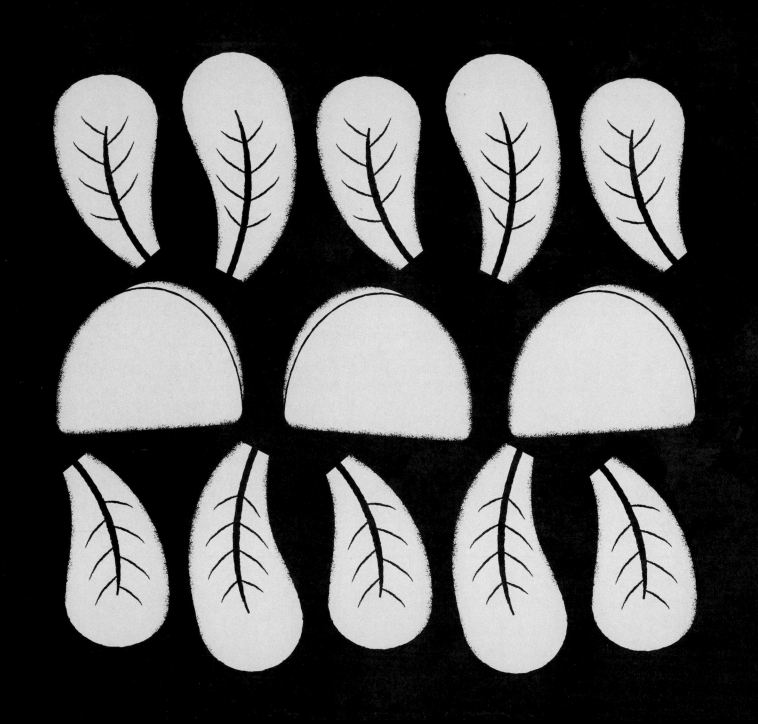

alternative banh mi

Vietnamese sandwiches have become so popular that many cooks are thinking beyond the traditional—without losing sight of what it is: a remarkable blending of culture, flavors, and textures. I hope these recipes inspire you to tinker beyond the pages of this book.

banh mi buns

Makes 16 large buns · **Takes about 1¹/₂ hours**

Following the trend of stuffing steamed buns with sliced pork belly, a number of chefs, including those at Saigon Sisters in Chicago, started stuffing *banh bao chay* (unfilled Chinese steamed buns) with banh mi ingredients. I haven't tried this with every banh mi filling in this book, but my gut tells me that the cold cuts wouldn't be great. But roasted or grilled meats work well, as does the Vietnamese pulled pork (page 90). Chinese Barbecued Pork (page 89; pictured at left) is a particular highlight. Experiment.

Use a moderate-protein flour like Gold Medal for great results; choose bleached flour for a lighter color and crumb, or unbleached for good flavor. Combining yeast with baking powder ensures the rise in the steamer.

1½ teaspoons instant (fast acting/rapid rise) dry yeast

¾ cup (180 ml) warm tap water (about 100°F / 38°C)

3 tablespoons canola oil

2 teaspoons baking powder

2 tablespoons sugar

2½ cups (12.5 oz / 350 g) bleached or unbleached all-purpose flour

Put the yeast in a small bowl or measuring cup and add the water. Let sit for 1 minute to soften, then whisk in 2 tablespoons of the oil. Set aside.

Put the baking powder, sugar, and flour in the work bowl of a food processor. Pulse 2 or 3 times to combine. Run the machine and pour the yeast mixture through the feed tube in a steady stream (start slowly and gradually pour faster). Keep the machine running until a large ball forms and cleans the sides of the bowl; expect some dangling bits. The finished dough should feel medium-soft and tacky, but not stick to your fingers.

Transfer the dough and bits to a work surface and give it a few turns to gather it into a neat ball; you shouldn't need any flour. If the dough feels tight, wet your hands and knead in the moisture. (To make the dough by hand see the Notes, page 118.)

Smear a little oil in a clean bowl and put the dough in it. Cover with plastic wrap and put in a warm place, such as an oven with the light on, to rise for 45 minutes, or until nearly doubled.

Meanwhile, cut 16 parchment paper squares, each about 3 inches (7.5 cm) wide. Have the remaining 1 tablespoon of oil and a pastry brush nearby.

Transfer the risen dough to a work surface—you should not need to flour it. Roll the dough into a long rope, about 2 inches (5 cm) thick and 16 inches (40 cm) long. Use a knife to cut it crosswise into 16 even pieces. Lightly roll each piece between your hands into a ball, then smack it with the palm of your hand into a disk about ⅓ inch (8 mm) thick.

continued

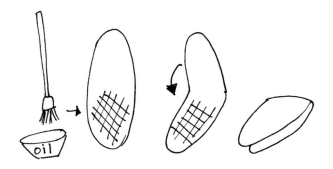

With a rolling pin, roll each dough piece into thin ovals, a good 5 by 3 inches (7.5 by 12.5 cm). Roll from the top down, or from the midline to the rim, and rotate often. Brush a little oil on half of the oval, then fold over.

Place on a parchment paper square and put in a bamboo or metal steamer tray, spacing them about 1 inch (2.5 cm) apart and away from the wall of the steamer. Repeat with the remaining dough pieces, putting overflow buns on a baking sheet after the steamer trays fill up.

Loosely cover the buns with a dry kitchen towel. Let rise in a warm spot for 20 to 30 minutes, until nearly doubled. Meanwhile, fill the steamer pan or a pot halfway with water and bring to a rolling boil over high heat. Lower the heat until you are ready to steam.

Steam the buns over boiling water, 1 or 2 trays at a time, rotating their positions midway, if needed, for 6 to 8 minutes, until puffy and dry looking. Keep in the steamer trays and use slightly warm or at room temperature. Or completely cool and freeze for up to 1 month; thaw and resteam or refresh in a microwave oven, covered by a damp paper towel.

NOTES

To assemble **banh mi buns**, open the rolls and moisten the top and bottom with cooking juices and/or mayonnaise. Add Maggi or another salty sauce. From the bottom up, stuff the buns with thin cucumber rounds, chile slices, the filling, pickle, and herb. This layering ensures that the bun will grip the ingredients well.

When making the dough by hand, soften the yeast in the water, then mix in the 2 tablespoons of oil. Put the remaining dry ingredients in a large bowl. Make a well in the center and pour in the yeast mixture. Stir with a wooden spoon from the center toward the rim to form a ragged, soft mass; add water by the teaspoon, if needed. Then use your fingers to gather and pat the dough together into a ball. Transfer to a work surface and knead for about 5 minutes, until smooth, soft, and a bit elastic. When pressed with a finger, the dough should spring back, with a faint indentation remaining. Follow the rest of the recipe as directed.

lettuce wrap banh mi

Serves 6 as a snack ▪ **Takes about 15 minutes**

Wrapping morsels of food in lettuce is a common Viet way of eating. One day while writing this book, I had a bunch of herbed salmon cakes (page 79) left over and a potluck to attend. So I brought an appetizer of lettuce wraps comprised of the cakes, banh mi vegetable accouterments, lettuce leaves, and *nuoc cham*, the basic Viet dipping sauce. It was a major hit. Nearly all of the fillings would work here. Use a reamer to juice the limes; the pulp lends body to the sauce. See the Note for a vegan dipping sauce.

Dipping Sauce

¼ cup (60 ml) fresh lime juice (from 2 or 3 limes)

2 teaspoons unseasoned rice vinegar (optional, to round out flavors)

2 tablespoons sugar

½ cup (120 ml) lukewarm water

About 3 tablespoons fish sauce

1 or 2 Thai or serrano chiles, thinly sliced

1 clove garlic, minced (optional)

A batch of banh mi filling of choice

1 regular cucumber or small English cucumber

16 to 20 sprigs of cilantro, mint, Thai basil, or other fresh herbs

1 head butter or other soft lettuce, leaves separated

1 cup (240 ml) pickles (choose from pages 33 to 37)

To make the dipping sauce, in a small bowl, combine the lime juice, vinegar, sugar, and water. Stir to dissolve the sugar. Taste and adjust the flavors to balance the sweet and sour. Add fish sauce to taste, aiming for a bold, tangy-salty flavor—the other ingredients are mostly unsalted. Add the chile and garlic (or serve the chiles on the side). Keep the sauce in a communal bowl for self-service, or portion it out in advance for serving. The sauce may be prepared early in the day and left at room temperature until serving.

Make the filling fresh or reheat and return it to room temperature; see individual recipes for guidance. Cut it into bite-size pieces and present on a plate.

Peel the cucumber, if you like. Halve it lengthwise, seed it, then cut it into thin crescents. Arrange with the herbs and lettuce on a platter. Set at the table with the sauce, filling, and pickles.

Invite guests to pick up or tear a palm-size piece of lettuce for each wrap and fill with 1 or 2 pieces of filling, pickle, cucumber, and herb leaves; tear up huge herb leaves and feel free to combine two or more types of herbs. Gather up the lettuce and dip in the sauce before eating.

NOTE

For a **vegan dipping sauce**, stir together 1 teaspoon of fine sea salt, 3 tablespoons of lime juice, 3 tablespoons of packed light palm sugar or brown sugar, ½ cup (120 ml) of lukewarm water, and 1 teaspoon of regular soy sauce. Taste and adjust the tangy-savory flavor before adding 1 small minced clove of garlic and 1 or 2 Thai or serrano chiles. Let sit for 10 minutes before using. If the filling you choose tastes good with the spicy hoisin sauce (page 31), use it instead.

banh mi salad

Makes 4 servings · **Takes about 30 minutes**

I'd been using a Marcella Hazan panzanella bread salad recipe for years before I realized that her Italian ideas could be applied to create a deconstructed banh mi salad. I simply swapped fish sauce for anchovies, Viet pickles for capers, pickling brine for vinegar, hot chile for sweet pepper, and Asian herbs for Italian basil. Marcella's recipe included cucumber, so I was set. Enjoy the salad alone for a light lunch or present it with one of the banh mi proteins for a filling meal. Or, cut up the protein, as tester Laura McCarthy suggested, and add it directly to the salad; leftovers would work too. Banh mi the salad is as flexible as banh mi the sandwich.

Half a baguette or 2 rolls suitable for banh mi

Salt, kosher preferred

About 6 tablespoons (90 ml) canola, grapeseed, or a mild-tasting olive oil

⅓ cup (90 ml) banh mi pickle (choose from pages 33 to 37)

¼ cup (60 ml) pickling brine (from the pickle)

2 teaspoons fish sauce, mock Maggi sauce (page 30), Maggi Seasoning sauce, or regular soy sauce

1 small clove garlic, minced and mashed or put through a garlic press

1 jalapeño or Fresno chile, chopped

8 ounces (225 g) cucumber, any kind

1 pound (450 g) juicy, ripe tomatoes

Pepper

A large handful of coarsely chopped fresh herbs, such as Thai or Italian basil, cilantro, and Vietnamese coriander (*rau ram*)

Position a rack in the middle of the oven and preheat to 350°F (180° or 175°C / gas mark 4). Use a serrated knife to cut the bread into ¾-inch (2-cm) cubes. Put into a large bowl and toss with a couple sprinklings of salt and 2 tablespoons of the oil. Spread out on a baking sheet and bake for 12 to 15 minutes, until crisp and golden. Let cool completely, about 15 minutes.

Meanwhile, use the bread bowl to prepare the rest of the salad. (If you're using the snow pea pickle, cut it into pieces to roughly match the bread.) Put the pickle in the bowl along with the pickling brine, fish sauce, garlic, chile, and 3 to 4 tablespoons of oil.

Peel the cucumber, if you like, then quarter it lengthwise. Seed the pieces, then cut them crosswise into ¼-inch (6-mm) thick fans. Add to the bowl.

If using cherry tomatoes, stem and halve each one before adding to the bowl. With other kinds of tomatoes, halve each, then seed them over the bowl (hold the tomato cut side down and squeeze gently) to release the gelatinous insides into the dressing. Cut the tomato into pieces to match the bread, then add them to the bowl. Season with salt and pepper. Finish the salad or set aside for up to 1 hour.

Shortly before serving, add the bread and herb to the tomato mixture. Toss well, then let sit for several minutes to allow flavors to meld. Taste and fine-tune by adding pickling brine and/or oil by the tablespoon. Divide among shallow soup bowls or plates and serve. If handy, garnish with sprigs of herb.

ACKNOWLEDGMENTS

I OFTEN THINK THAT I'M ONE OF THE LUCKIEST PEOPLE because I get to cook and write books, my dream job since I was ten years old. My parents Hoang and Tuyet Nguyen, husband Rory, and publisher Ten Speed Press indulge my curiosity and give me free rein, more or less, most of the time.

It was great fun to spend a year obsessing about banh mi, its traditional foundation as well as modern interpretations. Ten Speed Press—from publisher Aaron Wehner and editor Melissa Moore to marketing director Michelle Crim and art director Betsy Stromberg, hopped on board the banh mi train without hesitation. Melissa and publicist Kelly Snowden enthusiastically evaluated initial rounds of my banh mi rolls over cocktails. Hannah Rahill championed this work to book buyers large and small.

When it got to the nitty-gritty of recipe writing, I couldn't have asked for a better group of smart recipe testers, many of whom are veterans of my previous book projects. Work, vacation, the 2013 Boston bombing, and family matters didn't hinder the volunteers from thoughtfully tackling the recipes. A million thanks to this dedicated team of banh mi testers: Diane Carlson, Alex Ciepley, Jay Dietrich, Georgia Freedman-Wand, Alyce Gershenson, Petra Gördüren, Candace Grover, Doug Grover, Andrew Janjigian, Robyn Laing, Thien-Kieu Lam, Thien-Kim Lam, Kate Leahy, Laura McCarthy, Josie Nevitt, Karen Shinto, Terri Tanaka, Maki Tsuzuki, Dave Weinstein, and Lea Yancey.

Many friends old and new contributed information. Chefs Eric Banh, Bryant Ng, Alex Ong, and Diep Tran offered their banh mi creativity. Recovering from a stroke, Yun Ho Rhee sent a recipe from South Korea. Author Randy Clemens came to my rescue when I was looking for a tempeh banh mi. Master banh mi baker Ngoc Bui generously shared his life story. Mike Ly recounted technical tidbits from an impromptu baking lesson in Vietnam long ago. Hanoi-based Tracey Lister did reconnaissance work to help me better understand doner kebab banh mi.

Books are not made in a vacuum. This handsome publication benefited from captivating design by Betsy Stromberg, vivid photography by Paige Green, lyrical styling by Karen Shinto, and prop styling by Tessa Watson. Copyeditor Clancy Drake, proofreader Karen Levy, and indexer Ken Della Penta ensured that the words were as good as the images.

Thank you, everyone, for this collaboration.

INDEX

Published in the United States by Ten Speed Press, an
imprint of the Crown Publishing Group, a division of
Random House LLC, a Penguin Random House Company,
New York.
www.crownpublishing.com
www.tenspeed.com

Library of Congress Cataloging-in-Publication Data
is on file with the publisher.

Hardcover ISBN: 978-1-60774-533-4
eBook ISBN: 978-1-60774-534-1

Printed in China

Design by Betsy Stromberg
Food Styling by Karen Shinto
Prop Styling by Tessa Watson

10 9 8 7 6 5 4 3 2 1

First Edition